Shaping Catholic Parishes

Shaping Catholic Parishes

PASTORAL LEADERS IN THE TWENTY-FIRST CENTURY

Edited by Carole Ganim

◇◇◇

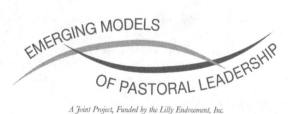

A Joint Project, Funded by the Lilly Endowment, Inc.

LOYOLA PRESS.
A JESUIT MINISTRY
Chicago

Partnering for Pastoral Excellence

    National Catholic Young Adult Ministry Association

National Association for Lay Ministry

Conference for Pastoral Planning and Council Development

National Association of Church Personnel Administrators

National Association of Diaconate Directors

National Federation of Priests Councils

LOYOLA PRESS.
A JESUIT MINISTRY

3441 N. Ashland Avenue
Chicago, Illinois 60657
(800) 621-1008
www.loyolapress.com

Cover design by Kathryn Seckman Kirsch
Interior design by Maggie Hong

Library of Congress Cataloging-in-Publication Data
Shaping Catholic parishes : pastoral leaders in the twenty-first century /
edited by Carole Ganim.
   p. cm.
 ISBN-13: 978-0-8294-2646-5
 ISBN-10: 0-8294-2646-9
 1. Parishes—United States—Case studies. 2. Catholic Church—United
States—Case studies. 3. Pastoral theology—United States—Case studies.
4. Pastoral theology—Catholic Church—Case studies. I. Ganim, Carole.
 BX1407.P3S53 2007
 250.88'28273—dc22

                                                    2007047236

Printed in the United States of America
08 09 10 11 12 13 Versa 10 9 8 7 6 5 4 3 2

Contents

IV. Pastoral

V. Prophetic

VI. Commentary

Foreword

Bishop Blase J. Cupich
Diocese of Rapid City
Rapid City, South Dakota

The Acts of the Apostles, scripture scholars tell us, is best understood in terms of its relationship to the Gospel of Luke. Just as the third evangelist recounts the life, death, and resurrection of Jesus as the one story of God fulfilling his promises, so too he relates what happens in the churches as the continuation of that one story.

That insight came to mind as I read these stories. This book belongs to the genre of acts, an "Acts of the Church in the United States." These accounts give us a snapshot of the life of the church in our day, complete with a full description of our wide diversity, of the enormous challenges we face in a new reality, and of the breadth of the talent that both the lay and the ordained bring to serving the people of God.

We have here the kind of eyewitness testimony found in the Acts of the Apostles. These brothers and sisters serve the church in this new reality relying not on their own initiative or on their own strengths, and surely not on a desire for personal gain. Rather, they come with a deep faith that what is happening in our Catholic Church through these emerging models of ministry is nothing less than the ongoing work of the risen Lord in our midst, to borrow from Luke.

These gifted and dedicated people share the common conviction that Christ is present, always exercising his priestly ministry, and that they are privileged to participate in this great work of redemption. It is a conviction that motivates them to collaborate with others in highly pluralistic and sometimes tense settings, to combine creativity and humility in rethinking how best to serve others, and to endure the suffering that comes from misunderstanding in a time of unparalleled transition.

Tensions and misunderstandings requiring clarification and deeper reflection on the tradition, voiced here by some, mirror what we read in Acts about the early church on pilgrimage. There we find communities in formation, facing questions as fundamental as whom to admit as their members. All of this argues for the need to invest the church's resources in formation programs for this generation of ecclesial ministers, thereby ensuring that the church fully benefits from their zeal for service.

Consideration of the attention given in these stories to promoting lay ministry in comparison with promoting ordained ministry offers a glimpse of today's tensions that need our further reflection. Father Anthony J. Pogorelc rightly remarks that none of the participants sets lay ministry in opposition to ordained ministry, and in fact, they value both. Yet the great enthusiasm for calling lay men and women to share their gifts in church ministry expressed here does not seem matched by a similar urge to invite young men to study for the priesthood. This is not to say that those interviewed are lukewarm or opposed to vocations to the priesthood. It does highlight an urgent need to promote in the church a sense of corporate responsibility for vocations and for addressing the serious shortage of priests. The church community is whole when Christians exercise their baptismal vocation and priests minister to them, in Christ's name, through their vocation to the ordained ministry. If a sense is lacking that we all share the task of promoting priestly vocations, we will be tempted to forget the intrinsic connection that exists between these two vocations and to make it a mere matter of changing church discipline. Perhaps the very awareness that we all have a stake in the future of the church, the same awareness that prompts these lay ministers to serve the church, is the place to start, a resource that has to be mined more deeply to avoid one-dimensional responses to the need for more priests.

Nonetheless, there is an authenticity to the acts recorded in this book that is compelling. It gives voice to our coworkers in the vineyard, who are dedicated to building the ecclesial communion entrusted to the care of bishops, one that "presupposes the participation of every category of the faithful, inasmuch as they share responsibility for the good of the particular Church which they themselves form" (Pope John Paul II to bishops from Pennsylvania and New Jersey, 2004 ad limina visit, citing *Pastores Gregis*, 44).

Finally, there is one other common denominator uniting these voices that is worthy of our attention and respect. These people love the church. As a result, they love what they do.

So, listen to these people speak. Share their conviction that Christ is alive and at work in our midst in the life of the church. Let them inspire you to love the church as they do.

Bishop Blase J. Cupich has been bishop of Rapid City in South Dakota, since 1998. He is currently chair of the U.S. Conference of Catholic Bishops' Vocations Committee and a member of the Bishops' Committee on the Liturgy and of the Ad Hoc Committee on Scripture Translation. He is the episcopal adviser to the Emerging Models of Pastoral Leadership Project.

Introduction

Carole Ganim

Telling the stories of other people implies a certain empathy and ability to practice what John Keats called negative capability, a receptivity and loss of self in order to transmit the truth and art of another. Having tried earnestly to practice these virtues and to present the voice of the speaker as truthfully as possible while writing and editing these stories, I now find it difficult to step out of that role and speak in my own voice. It is true, however, that I have had a wonderful time doing this work, and I do have a story about how the book came together.

The Emerging Models of Pastoral Leadership Project studied pastoral ministry in Catholic parishes in the United States. As part of the research, participants conducted a series of regional symposia, which were designed to review, evaluate, and anticipate future models for leadership in local churches. Dioceses selected pastoral leaders, both clerical and lay, to participate in one of the eight regional leadership symposia. At each symposium, people listened to speakers, told their stories, tried to capture and evaluate what was happening in parish ministry, and shared ideas and problems. They worked to understand the underlying issues and spiritual and societal forces influencing the church and its people and to define parish life and pastoral leadership as they were and as they should be. The participants shared their stories with one another, compared notes on the nature of parish work, prayed and laughed together, and talked about the current and future state of the church. My part of the process began when I attended one of the regional symposia. I got a strong sense of groundedness and enthusiasm from the participants. At a time of tension within the church, these men and women were moving ahead, joyfully and seriously.

After all the symposia had concluded, Marti Jewell, the director of the Emerging Models project, and David Ramey, consultant and facilitator of the symposia, drew up a list of potential contributors to this book, one of a series of books about the project. They used such criteria as region, gender, function, ethnicity, age, and others in an attempt to fairly represent the spectrum of parish ministry throughout the country. The ministers and their stories included here represent the diversity of the American Catholic experience. This book was to present the real people of the church, in their own voices, and in their own idiosyncratic personhood. My challenge was to put it together.

I began by calling or e-mailing all the people on the list to set up a phone interview. Most people were honored and happy to participate. In fact, throughout the process, I had excellent cooperation from each person. Everyone responded quickly and patiently to the many phone calls, e-mails, questions, and concerns that I had. I then sent each a list of questions to look at before the interview in order to have a more focused conversation. Being a technological wizard, I set up a small tape recorder next to my computer and placed my phone on speaker between the two. I assumed this high-level technological feat would produce high-fidelity transmission. Actually, the arrangement worked quite well, except when I forgot to start the tape or when I did not notice that the tape was becoming twisted, because I was busy taking notes and being absorbed in the conversation. The interviews were the most fun. I talked to each person several times and felt that I got to know each one. Each story was fascinating and inspirational. Here were ordinary people doing day-to-day things in ordinary ways, ways that added up to the extraordinary. Here were people like the people in the Gospel stories, the folk of the community tending to their own.

I learned many things from my informants. I learned about the multitude of names for people doing parish ministry: parish life coordinator, pastoral associate, deacon, canonical pastor, youth minister, adult minister, pastoral life director, and so on. I learned a little about parish politics, about differences in diocesan practices, about parish councils, about getting out the bulletin and maintaining the Web site. I learned about these accidentals in the course of the conversations, but they led me to observe that church and parish language has its own separate existence. Like every other argot associated with a job or a culture, parish culture creates its own vocabulary to describe its own reality.

Most of all, I learned that clerical and lay ecclesial ministry is flourishing in the church. The composite presents a vibrant, optimistic picture of parish life today and a promise of continuous development of the church and parish. The U.S. Conference of Catholic Bishops' 2005 publication *Co-workers in the Vineyard of the Lord: A Resource for Guiding the Development of Lay Ecclesial Ministry* ratifies the promise inherent in these pages: "Ministry in the Church continues the ministry of Jesus through the ages and throughout the world. Continually the Spirit calls forth new ministries and new ministers to serve evolving needs, as the history of the Church shows."

I was also struck by the amazing consistency among the participants' stories. Some feel they were called, others speak of a gradual movement toward ministry, a few even were gently coerced, but all express their sense of vocation, or responding to a need in the community and a willingness to serve God. Uniformly, they stressed the importance of relationship, a tangible relationship with Jesus and with their parishioners. To me, they exemplify the meaning of minister, one who is subordinate to a master or magister, and thus one who serves. They are humble in the best sense of the word because they see their role as servant, and they are servant-leaders. They are characteristically both proud of their successes and accomplishments and quick to turn the attention from themselves in order to praise the work of the parishioners or others who work with them. They are interested in people, not power and certainly not acquisition. I suspect that the Home Shopping Network doesn't take up too much of their time. Not one person cares about money as a personal goal or value, although some mention the need for church funding. Most of the speakers are open about their own weaknesses, which makes them refreshingly human. They emphatically practice the works of mercy and justice without fanfare. They are good people without guile.

The Emerging Models of Pastoral Leadership Project began in 2003 with the expectation of discovering and discussing a variety of structural models that are being created to provide for parish life in the United States. The research has found that there has been and continues to be evolving structural change in pastoral leadership and an emerging model of pastoral leadership, which these stories represent.

Early in the study, marks of excellence were identified as ways of describing and defining the characteristics of pastoral leaders and leadership. The stories told here are organized according to these marks of excellence: collaborative, ethical, pastoral, prophetic, and welcoming. Each individual's story is rich and complex and cannot be reduced to a single characteristic; in fact, the marks of excellence can be found in all the stories, but we have chosen to emphasize a certain aspect in each story and have grouped them accordingly.

Part 1, "Welcoming," focuses on parishes in which issues of difference and diversity exist. Pastoral leaders have a warmth and generosity of spirit that creates an environment of acceptance and a celebration of differences.

Part 2, "Collaborative," focuses on larger parishes or parish clusters that have learned ways to collaborate within the parish, or within a group of parishes, and with both lay and clerical ministers. These stories stress the virtues of the collaborator: patience, organization, and strength.

Part 3, "Ethical," focuses on parishes with overwhelming demands and difficult decisions facing the pastoral ministers. The stories here emphasize the ethical aspect of ministry; that is, the necessity of an authentic person ministering to others and influencing personal relationships within the community.

Part 4, "Pastoral," focuses on rural parishes in relatively isolated places and the stresses and joys associated with rural ministry. The pastoral presence in rural communities is often, but not always, best filled by someone with deep roots in the community and an understanding of the local culture.

Part 5, "Prophetic," focuses on parishes facing crises or unique situations that call for inspired leadership. These pastoral ministers respond and act with vision and clarity to a call they did not necessarily seek.

Immersed as I was in the individuals and their stories, I was glad to get three objective analyses of their totality. The theological perspective presented by Zeni Fox and the sociologist's commentary offered by Father Anthony Pogorelc helped me see the experiences in a larger context. Donna Markham, OP, is a psychologist who underscores the transformative leadership exemplified in the stories. Each of them stresses the dynamism of the church as it is embodied in the leaders who are speaking. Each sees the present manifestation of church development as historically consistent and a reflection of deep faith.

Anthony Pogorelc stresses the four pillars of priestly formation identified by Pope John Paul II—human, spiritual, intellectual, and pastoral—as identifiers of all ministers and goes on to analyze the ministers in this context. Zeni Fox frames her analysis by asking the question, How is this change consonant with the tradition of the church? In answering the question, she discusses diversity and collaboration in ministry as exemplified in the stories and looks at future challenges inherent in them. Donna Markham names the qualities of transformative leadership—community, connection, and collaboration—and says that all must be present for change and growth to occur. She then asks three questions: Whose parish is it? Who has authority to make decisions? and How will conflicts be resolved?

These voices are voices of the living church and of the Spirit. They tell us what we need to know about church and community, love and holiness, along with the good old-fashioned virtues of diligence, perseverance, and hard work. They are the reality that embodies the theories; they are the praxis that demonstrates the principles. They are the best of the Catholic Church today. It has been my privilege to help these people tell their stories.

I
WELCOMING

Welcoming leaders ensure that all who desire a closer relationship to God are genuinely received and welcomed, in a spirit of heartfelt hospitality, openness, and eagerness both to give and to receive. They are also inclusive leaders, who invite, support, and animate diversity in the parish, paying particular attention to diverse cultures, languages, ethnicities, gender, generations, abilities, and beliefs, in ways that are respectful and mutually enriching.

An Anglo-Hispanic parish flourishes in Seattle

"I tell the people, 'I'm sorry, but when I was sent to you, it put you on the cutting edge.'"

Patty Repikoff
Pastoral Life Director
Christ the King/Cristo Rey Parish
Seattle, Washington

Parish Profile: Christ the King/Cristo Rey parish includes about nine hundred English-speaking and one thousand Hispanic families, as well as a parochial school. The parish serves a nearby hospital, retirement homes, and assisted-living facilities.

◇◇◇

At St. Therese, my first parish, we built a ministry based on baptism. I was a pastoral leader shaped not by holy orders but by baptism, and I invited everyone to exercise their baptismal call with me. I believe that my skills and background in spirituality and liturgy, catechesis, action for justice, pastoral care, and Catholic education served to enhance that community, and together we built a strong body of witnesses to the gospel.

I worked to ensure that the community members were well formed as pastoral ministers. I spent two years training a cadre of parish leaders so that they could preside at rituals that did not require a priest. I wanted to use my time there to form them into a confident and adult church. The church doubled in size during the eight years I was there.

In 1998, I went to Christ the King/Cristo Rey Church with a new title, pastoral life director. I still hold that title. The role of pastoral life director is disappearing in our diocese; there are only two, both women, remaining.

The ministerial responsibilities did not change, but the title did. I was still appointed by the archbishop to serve as the pastoral leader of the parish and to collaborate in ministry with the two priests assigned to preside at sacraments. I oversee the pastoral life of the community. We have about nine hundred English-speaking and about one thousand Hispanic families, in addition to a parochial school (pre-school to eighth grade), a nearby hospital, retirement homes, and assisted-living facilities. My title is "Patty," and the priests and I work as a team. One of the priests serves the Spanish-speaking community on the weekends, and the English-speaking priest is present most of the time. As at St. Therese, I take an active part in the weekend liturgies and preach regularly.

One of my deepest hopes as pastoral life director is to change the hearts and minds of the people so that they can really become church rather than just go to church. I find my hope in the commitment to the people and in the people's commitment to building church. The words of Albert Nolan, OP, from his recent book *Jesus Today*, reflect my mission: "Jesus came not to turn the world upside down, but to turn it right side up."

At Christ the King/Cristo Rey Church, things were very rocky during the first months of my assignment. Eight months before I came, their beloved priest-pastor had died, and they received a promise that they would get a new priest as pastor. To them I was a slap in the face. It was a brutal beginning for both them and me. Their anger, directed at me, became my teacher. I struggled to respond on a higher level, but it was hard. I told them I understood that they had been poorly treated and asked them how I could love them.

For the first year, I didn't do much else but listen and be present. I also engaged in a deliberate prayer campaign. I began a practice that I still use. Every night I would pray for the people on one page of the parish directory. I also asked people to pray for one page each night. This helped me not only to get to know the parishioners but also to plant the idea of prayer as a path together in the parish. People were floored that I was praying for them and asking them to pray for one another. Over time, things improved. Some people said they were sorry. Some were grateful that I had never fought back. Now in my ninth year, most people have come around. A few have left the parish, but many new families have joined the parish.

Some of our accomplishments of the past few years of building a parish are bringing the Hispanic and English-speaking communities together for prayer, celebration, and service; starting the *Spiritual Exercises* of St. Ignatius of Loyola for fifty lay leaders, twenty-five English-speaking and twenty-five Spanish-speaking; adopting a sister parish in New Orleans post-Katrina; and sending forty people to New Orleans for the past two years to help our sister parish rebuild. I have worked especially hard to help new lay leaders to see themselves as ministers on the cutting edge. I tell them, "I'm sorry, but when I was sent to you, it put you on the cutting edge, even though you might not have been ready for it." The Ignatian exercises have been especially formative for our lay leaders, as we have found that running a parish is like running a retreat.

I believe that Christ the King/Cristo Rey is an emerging pastoral model in several ways:

- People have created their church together and will keep doing so.
- Because our church has both English- and Spanish-speaking people together, people have to learn to live with diversity and to appreciate different cultures.
- For some Spanish-speaking people, this is the first real experience with lay ministry and being church.
- The Hispanic Initiative at Christ the King School has opened up our parochial school to the participation of the children of the Spanish-speaking immigrants of Cristo Rey. We worked to integrate the children into the school in an intentional and programmatic way.

In other words, Christ the King/Cristo Rey is a model for what the U.S. church can become. The people of the parish are on the cutting edge in their acceptance of me, a nonordained woman, as their leader, their acceptance of a lay-priest pastoral team, and their acceptance of one another and the diversity of our community. We are building a strong church together.

Patty Repikoff has been active in parish ministry for more than twenty years. She was parochial minister at St. Therese Church in Seattle, a nine-hundred-family multicultural community, and was pastoral life director at Christ the King/Cristo Rey Parish. She is now coordinator of Hispanic ministry for the Eastside Deanery of the Seattle Archdiocese, which involves fourteen parishes and more than twenty thousand Hispanic Catholics.

In San Francisco, a church full of young adults

"We seem to be returning to the way it used to be, as laypeople take pivotal roles in helping shape and support their parish communities."

John J. Brust
Parishioner
St. Vincent de Paul Church
San Francisco, California

Parish Profile: St. Vincent de Paul is a parish of some 2,400 households in the Marina/Pacific Heights district of San Francisco. It has an especially active young-adult community.

◇◇◇

Attend Sunday 5:15 p.m. Mass at St. Vincent de Paul in San Francisco and you will find a church filled with young adults in their twenties and thirties being served by lectors, eucharistic ministers, and ushers of the same age. With all the doors leading to one area in front of the church, it is perfectly designed for these young adults to meet and congregate after Mass; and they often do for long periods of time, before making their way home or down the street for dinner.

I found St. Vincent de Paul Parish shortly after moving to San Francisco in late 2001 by thumbing through the Yellow Pages in search of the nearest Catholic church. I stumbled on to a gold mine rich in faith, service, and community.

St. Vincent's has one of the most active and vibrant groups of Catholic young adults in the Archdiocese of San Francisco and greater California.

Today, young adults can find the parish (and our young adult group) on the Internet (at www.svdpsf.org) and stay current with activities by visiting our Web site or subscribing to the weekly e-newsletter. The core activities of the group are the Monday evening speaker events that can draw more than one hundred young adults, depending on the guest speaker or topic. These events have brought speakers including Cardinal William Levada, Archbishop George Niederauer, Mayor Gavin Newsom, and Ninth Circuit Court of Appeals Judge Carlos Bea, and our topics range from relationships to current events.

It's far more than just these events, though, that have kept young adults coming back. The success of our group comes from providing a balance of spiritual, social, and service-oriented activities for Catholics in their twenties and thirties, and from having a pastor, Father John K. Ring, who offers our community his complete support. St. Vincent de Paul has the kind of faith community that some of us left behind in our hometowns or at our universities. It provides a place to learn, to develop friendships in a parish community, and to recharge one's spiritual batteries (through our annual young-adult retreat or weekly small faith groups), as well as a path for young Catholics looking for a transition back to the church.

In keeping with the work-life balance that our community of young professionals seeks, our group hosts a number of social events, including hikes in nearby parks, evenings at Giants baseball games, and wine-and-cheese socials, to compliment parish events (including the popular Mardi Gras party and black-tie Noel Ball). In addition, each year we organize a wine-bike trip in Napa Valley, a ski weekend in Lake Tahoe, a camping trip in Yosemite National Park with another young-adult group from a nearby parish, and the list goes on.

As is true with all of St. Vincent's parish groups (seniors, parents' guild, men's club, etc.), community service is an integral part of our young adult group. Our Thanksgiving food-delivery program brings together upward of forty young adults to deliver approximately 160 meals to needy families. Our Operation Easter Bunny (the brainchild of one of our young adults) puts Easter baskets into the hands of numerous less privileged children. And on a weekly basis, young adults teach classes at the parish school through the Junior Achievement Program, deliver fresh fruit to the needy, serve meals to the homeless, and visit the elderly.

Organizationally, our group is designed so that everyone takes a part of the ownership. Our activities (spiritual, social, and service) are organized and run by volunteers from our young adult community and not by a small group of designated leaders. While we do have a formalized leadership team, we are simply a steering committee (without titles), responsible for guiding our group in the right direction and encouraging others to step forward and lead activities that interest them most.

Regarding communication, we have found that embracing and making intelligent use of the Internet adds a great deal of value to a parish and its communities. We worked under this premise when we redesigned the parish Web site in 2004. The architectural plan for our site (parish and young adults combined) borrowed the best elements from parish Web sites across the country and brought them into a clean, functional, and tasteful layout. Our Web site now offers online parish registration, interactive maps, an easy-to-navigate activities calendar, and photo albums of events and participants, which encourages our young adults to return to the site on a regular basis.

With all of these activities and the benefits of technology, we hope to transition our young adults into active members and leaders of the parish. This is our church now and it's our responsibility to use our talents as best we can to meet the challenges of today's church.

My transition into parish ministry was an honest one, as I feel it's partly in my blood; but as I look back to my relatives, it's easy to see that each generation before us has had to face great challenges in the church of their day.

For example, my great-great-great-grandfather Nicholas Brust and his brother John Baptist Brust emigrated from Ulmen, Germany, in 1842 and 1843, at a time when Catholic churches were yet to be built in many towns. Nicholas settled in Milwaukee, and, as the stories were written, had to travel five miles to St. Stephen's Catholic Church by horse and buggy with his family each Sunday. John Baptist settled in an area north of Milwaukee (now Johnsburg) and, according to a historical marker in front of St. John the Baptist Church, would invite Catholics to gather at his home on Sundays and holy days for community prayer before the church was built.

Nicholas's son Christopher and grandson Peter Brust recognized this need for places of prayer and used their talents to design more than fifty churches, rectories, schools, seminaries, convents, and chapels. One of Peter's brothers, Nicholas, chose the priesthood and used his talents serving as the procurator for St. Francis Seminary in Milwaukee for twenty-five years. Another brother, Frank, had a son, Leo, who also entered the priesthood and rose to the position of auxiliary bishop for the Wisconsin Archdiocese. Following in Peter's footsteps, his two sons, John and Paul, and my father, David, also became architects and continued working closely with the needs of church.

I'm not an architect of buildings, but I feel blessed to have found St. Vincent de Paul, where I've been able to use my talents to help design our parish Web site and, along with my colleagues in ministry, build a community of young adults who identify with the needs of the church and their parish.

When I'm asked if I worry about the future of the Catholic Church, my answer is no. I see the church as being in an ongoing cycle of renewal. And right now, there seems to be a great desire in young adults to incorporate a spiritual component into their lives. We seem to be returning to the way it used to be, as laypeople take pivotal roles in helping shape and support their parish communities. We all have a small sense of responsibility to continue God's work as we have been called to do in our baptism and confirmation. In San Francisco, at St. Vincent de Paul, this sentiment is alive and well.

John J. Brust serves on the steering committee for the young adult group at St. Vincent de Paul Church and on the Archdiocesan Pastoral Council. He has spoken at national conferences and on radio and podcast programs on the use of technology in parish and young adult ministry. He is currently consulting on a project to redesign the Archdiocese of San Francisco's Web site. He has an MBA from the University of Notre Dame and works in the high-tech industry as a director of product marketing.

Pastoring diversity

*"I often feel like I am doing a juggling act
with the diversities of race, nationality,
background, language, age and gender.
Our constant mantra is that as we gather
around the altar we are one."*

Father Gregory Hartmayer, OFM Conv.
Pastor
St. Philip Benizi Church
Jonesboro, Georgia

Parish Profile: St. Philip Benizi Church is a growing, very diverse parish of about 2,500 families in the Atlanta suburbs. The congregation includes large numbers of Spanish-speaking, African, African American, and Filipino Catholics, as well as Caucasian Catholics who have relocated to the South.

◇◇◇

I came to St. Philip Benizi Church after the sudden death of the parish's pastor. I had never been an assistant in a parish before, much less a pastor. Yet here I was, not only a pastor but a pastor of a mega-church, a church of 2,500 families, with as diverse a population as could be found and a flourishing community whose previous pastor had been their leader and friend. Furthermore, the former pastor had been my very good friend and I was grieving too. It was strange to follow him, to live in his room and to minister to his flock. When the people of the church, however, realized that their new pastor shared and understood their grief, a bond formed between us.

I started the only way I knew how—by listening and watching. This was my first parish. I had nothing to compare it to. I saw people taking charge and I thought that this parish was like a well-oiled machine. There were dozens of keys out, a kind of symbol that the people were, in fact, the leaders and shepherds.

I learned a bit of the history. Atlanta Archbishop James Lyke, OFM, had asked the Conventual Franciscans, my community, to assume the parish in 1991. The church had a large debt; unhappiness and division were rife; and the parish was broken. Father Patrick Mendola, OFM Conv., became pastor in 1991 together with two other friars as parochial vicars, and things turned around. The tone of the parish changed. Father Mendola inaugurated parishwide listening sessions and fostered a spirit of collegiality. The people were empowered to take ownership of the church. The Sunday offertory increased. The church went off in a different direction. Then, three and a half years later, Father Mendola died. He was only forty-seven.

St. Philip Benizi is a large church fifteen miles south of downtown Atlanta. We have 2,500 families with a great diversity. About twenty-seven percent of the parish is Spanish-speaking people from more than a dozen different countries. In addition, forty-five percent of our congregation members are Caucasian, most of whom have migrated from other places primarily because of employment. We also have a large Filipino population, Africans from such places as Togo, Ghana, Nigeria, and Cameroon, and African American people who grew up in the rural South. We have two hundred fifty baptisms per year and twenty-five funerals. We also have an influx-outflow of some two hundred families per year, with a constant base of seven hundred to eight hundred families over a ten-year period. We also have a high number of converts, usually about twenty to thirty per year. In the Archdiocese of Atlanta, there are about two thousand converts every Easter. The demographics also point to the changes the church is facing in the South: growth, diversity, and multiculturalism.

The Spanish-speaking community is a microcosm of the parish. Most are from Mexico, but many other Spanish-speaking countries are represented. Parishioners from each country have a different culture, speak a different Spanish dialect, celebrate different feast days and holidays, play and dance to different music. They recognize the differences among themselves very well. There are, of course, tensions, but in the parish they work toward leading a gospel-centered life and enjoy celebrating the Eucharist together.

I encourage all ethnic groups to celebrate their culture, but sometimes there is a sense of competition. Each group meets as a group once a month. They want to pass their culture on to their children. They choose leaders who are their liaison to the parish. My job is to be understanding, supportive, and attentive to their sensitivities. As pastor, I often feel like I am doing a juggling act with the diversities of race, nationality, background, language, age, and gender. Our constant mantra is that we are one faith and as we gather around the altar we are one. It is our common faith that brings us together as one parish.

We strive to live by our mission statement:

St. Philip Benizi Catholic Church is dedicated to continuing the mission of Jesus Christ.

Endowed with the gifts of the Holy Spirit, we experience and express the presence of God through prayer, the celebration of the sacraments, and communal life.

We are a multicultural and diverse community united by our faith in God, by our desire to live the Gospel Message and by our Roman Catholic Tradition.

Aware that Baptism calls us all to active participation, we commit ourselves to the development of lay leadership and lay ministry.

We strive to be a strong and joyful sign of the Kingdom of God by spreading the Good News, serving those in need, growing spiritually and living Christ's Commandment of Love.

St. Philip Benizi is structured around the pastoral council and its five commissions. Every bona fide organization and ministry falls under one of the commissions. The commission model works well in a large church. Our pastoral council operates from the people's agenda from an annual town hall meeting each September. The people bring to the appropriate commission things they see from the pew and items they perceive as needing action. For instance, a railing was added to the three steps in the sanctuary because a few of the older lectors had trouble climbing the steps. In another situation, people observed that there was no forum for the senior members of our parish community, so a senior group was formed that meets monthly for recreation and prayer. The agenda proposals must go through the process of being presented first to the appropriate commission, then the pastoral council and then the pastoral staff before a proposal is approved. The commission model is a different way to run a parish and it works well for us. Things get done because they are planned, talked about, and acted upon by the people. The commission members are the living representation of the empowerment of the people.

Within the total parish, we have micro-communities in that people choose one of the seven weekend liturgies on the basis of their affiliations. Many seniors prefer the Saturday evening and early Sunday morning Mass because the time is convenient for them, but mainly because the service is more traditional with a cantor, organist, and more traditional music. Parents with children tend to worship during the midmorning Sunday Masses. Our teenagers enjoy the Life Teen Mass late Sunday afternoon. The Masses celebrated in Spanish are provided at midday and early evening on Sunday. Once a year, we really celebrate our diversity with a large parish multicultural Mass. We usually have about 1,500 people in attendance at the Mass and after Mass we have a festival of food from about twenty-five countries. We were honored to welcome Archbishop Wilton Gregory to celebrate with us last year.

St. Philip Benizi is a parish in which the people have a genuine concern for one another's welfare. It is not just a facade. A recent convert to Catholicism was in need of a kidney transplant and a much younger parishioner became aware of this need and volunteered to donate one of his kidneys. He was a perfect match. A successful kidney transplant followed. Last year, the forty-nine-year-old father of a family with six children died suddenly. The parish community took over and helped the family. These are not isolated examples, but rather the norm for the kind of ministry that is experienced within this parish.

We are not without our challenges. Some are based on growth and diversity issues. Finances are always a struggle. In recent years, we have experienced white flight of some families who have moved farther into the suburbs while newly married and low-income families have moved into our area. New immigrants and undocumented people not only have fewer resources but also often come from developing countries and feel they have an obligation to send support to their families back home. Another concern we are addressing with some of our new immigrants is to help change the thinking that the priest does everything and that the people come to church to fulfill a church obligation. Our parish is a prime example of the opposite, and most people eventually come to accept the responsibility of their baptismal promises as members of the community of the church. It is encouraging and gratifying to see ownership and leadership blossoming in most of the ethnic groups.

In the next three years, we will focus on evangelization and stewardship. We need to redefine and set new goals according to our mission and our developing parish.

I have been ordained twenty-eight years, and over the past twelve years, I am still learning about what it means to be a priest. And I am learning it from the people.

Father Gregory J. Hartmayer, OFM Conv., is the pastor of St. Philip Benizi Catholic Church and the Guardian of the Friars. Ordained in 1979, he came to St. Philip in 1995 after a career in secondary education.

A charismatic deacon in Amarillo

"Every Mass is a healing Mass because Jesus is there."

Deacon Pedro Juarez
Parish Life Coordinator
Diocese of Amarillo
Amarillo, Texas

Parish Profile: Deacon Juarez pastors three parishes in the Diocese of Amarillo with 1,900 total members. Most of the parishioners are Mexican.

◇◇◇

I had a strong call to full-time ministry. After I was ordained a permanent deacon, I had dreams about job offers. One dream that kept coming back was an offer from the Diocese of Amarillo. I knew the bishop in Amarillo and I liked him, so I went and presented myself to him. He said he had never had a full-time deacon but told me to wait. I waited five months and I went to the bishop again. By this time, I had quit my job, had two girls still at home, and my wife was getting desperate. I started the next week.

The bishop got me a house, paid the rent, and paid me a little bit of money. Because I could speak Spanish, I was a big help to the priest. The church was in Wellington and it was very empty, so I started knocking on doors and inviting the people to come to church. After five years, we had ten converts and two hundred people in church. Even non-Catholics would call and ask me to pray for them.

Now I am living in Silverton and I am the parish life coordinator for three parishes: San Loreto in Silverton, which has about 900 people; San Juan Diego in Quitaque, about 500; and San Elizabeth Seton in Turkey, about 500 people. In these churches, the people are mostly Mexican. A priest comes almost every Sunday to my parishes to say Mass. A deacon is almost like a priest, but I cannot consecrate, give absolution, or anoint the sick. I am getting paid like a priest now, though.

What I do is go to the people and pray for them and with them. The Good Lord calls me to pray for the sick. Some have diseases like cancer or high blood pressure that the doctors say is incurable. But I say that Jesus is a doctor and he's the only one who can decide what the last word is and can heal them. When I pray for them, some of them have been healed, even from cancer. Some people are depressed and they say they never have peace inside, but many healings have taken place when we pray for them. Our people pray for the needs of those who are sick, who have no hope. The Lord wants us to believe every word that he says. Jesus is the same yesterday, today, and tomorrow.

Most of our parishioners are from Mexico and came here because they wanted better jobs and opportunities for their families. The diocese is generous and tries to help them get papers, and I try to help them too. I try to minister to them in the way they are used to, but sometimes I have to tell them that we are in a different country now and we can't keep all our celebrations or all of our ways. One of the most popular activities for the people is sports. On Saturdays and Sundays, they play football or soccer, and it is a big family and community event. There are food and drinks and games and the people love it. Sometimes they don't come to church on those days. I try to tell them that the Lord comes first and I even have communion early, but that doesn't always work. It's a family day and they have a good time. I try to be patient.

We are lucky here because we have few problems with our teenagers, no gangs, and not much trouble. In the bigger cities like Albuquerque or Plainview, gangs are a serious problem.

I feel blessed because the Lord is calling me to serve. The Lord is opening all the closed doors. I believe in a strong way in the Eucharist and in healing and reconciliation. I have Bible classes once a week, and I share the faith with the people. I start teaching them Catholic doctrine—about the Eucharist, the rosary, and the healing of the sick. Many of the people have been to Protestant churches. They come back and they want to know why we Catholics believe what we do. I take them to the Bible, to the Catechism, and explain step-by-step. They are grateful because nobody has explained these things to them before.

I conduct many communion services in my three churches because of the shortage of priests. Sometimes we don't know how lucky we are in the United States. In Mexico, one priest often has sixteen parishes.

Every week I am in all three parishes. On Monday, I go to Quitaque; on Tuesday, to Silverton; and on Wednesday, I am in Turkey. I visit the sick, take communion to the sick and the elderly, help families prepare for the baptism of their children, and try to meet the needs of the people. About 4 p.m. we have adoration of the Blessed Sacrament, and then we have Bible study and apologetics for one or two hours. About twelve to fifteen people come after they have spent the day at work on the farm. Thursday is usually my day off. I work in the yard and then my wife, Teresa, and I might go out to eat and relax.

I go once a month to do retreats for people. The retreats are about marriage, healing, and reconciliation. I believe in the power of the Eucharist and the power of healing, and I have seen healing right there when we are praying together.

Sometimes what I do is hard on my family. My wife helps me in the church with teaching and especially marriage preparation classes, and my daughter helps with the music. We have instrumental music and we use karaoke. But sometimes my girls ask, "Why do you have to be in the church all the time?"

At first, I had some problems with some of the Anglos who didn't want to accept me. They had a different view about what the church should be. Some of them would not even shake my hand at the sign of peace. I asked the Lord to use me to reach out to everyone and I tried to talk to them. For five years, I just kept asking them to greet me at the sign of peace. Finally it worked. I knew that the love of Jesus would work. When I left that parish, a lot of those people came to me and told me that I really taught them a lot. I asked them why, and they said that I taught them about the love of Jesus because they rejected me, but I kept loving them. I said, "Well, praise God!" Now these people always ask me for baptisms and always call me to help them.

When I went recently to one of our churches to talk about the Eucharist, I noticed that the people were sitting in the back of the church. I asked them if they stay in the back or come up close when they go to a concert or to see somebody famous. They said they like to be real close. So I said if we believe that Jesus is in the Eucharist, then we should want to be close to him. So everybody moved up to the front pews. I say to them that if we believe that Jesus is in the Eucharist, we can't only believe; we have to act on it. Every Mass is a healing Mass because Jesus is there. We have a good time at Mass because people believe that Jesus is really in the Eucharist.

We need more deacons and laypeople to serve in the church. As a deacon, I have to prepare the people to serve the church and the Lord. I know that you don't have to be very educated to serve in the church. I only finished the sixth grade, but there are many places for everybody. If the church needs someone for a certain job, then the church can call that person and can train them. People who want to serve can serve even if they don't have much education. People want to do what the Lord calls them to do.

Espanol

Les saluda el diácono Pedro Juárez, de la diócesis de Amarillo, Texas. Quiero compartir con ustedes lo que está haciendo el Señor Jesucristo en la parroquia del Santísimo Sacramento.

El día 10 de junio fui invitado a dar una enseñanza tocante al Cuerpo y la Sangre de Cristo Jesús. Al llegar a la iglesia donde iba a dar esta enseñanza, me di cuenta de que toda la gente estaba sentada atrás. Mi pregunta fue esta. Si de veras creemos que Cristo está presente en el Santísimo sacramento, ¿por qué no nos acercamos más a él?

Cuando vamos a un baile amenizado por un grupo famoso, todos queremos estar en las primeras filas. ¿Por qué no lo hacemos con Cristo Jesús, esto es, querer estar cerca de él?

Aquí está presente el Santísimo Sacramento. Además, en muchos otros lugares hay muchas personas que hablan muy bonito acerca de Cristo Jesús. Pero aquí no nada más hablamos de él, sino que él está presente aquí, en el Santísimo Sacramento.

Ya para despedirnos vino una señora, preguntándonos si podíamos orar por otra persona que se había lastimado la espalda y no podía moverse. Le dijimos que sí y fuimos a ella. Al estar orando hubo un momento en el que la presencia de Cristo fue tan real que se podía experimentar de una manera muy fuerte, y fue así que le dije a la hermana: "Muévete, ya estás sana. Cristo te ha sanado". Y empezó a correr y brincar alabando a Cristo Jesús, porque ya no le dolía nada.

Gracias a Cristo Jesús. Que Cristo los bendiga. Son los deseos de su hermano en Cristo,

Diácono Pedro Juárez y familia

Deacon Pedro Juarez was born in Guanajuato, Mexico, in 1954 and came to the United States in 1971 to find work. He settled in Houston, raised a family, and worked for many years at Levi Strauss. He was ordained a permanent deacon in the Diocese of Lubbock in 1996 and has worked in full-time ministry ever since.

Laotian, Catholic, and American

*"The biggest problems have to do with the
change in culture. The Lao people have to adapt
to a new society."*

Deacon Joua Pao Yang
Pastoral Coordinator to the Lao Tribal
Community
Seattle, Washington

Parish Profile: Deacon Joua Pao Yang serves the Lao tribal community
in the Archdiocese of Seattle from a base at Our Lady of Mount Virgin
parish in Seattle.

◇◇◇

When the North Vietnamese completely took over Laos in
1975, I took my family across the Mekong River into Thailand
in a small boat when the soldiers who guarded the Mekong's
shore went to lunch. When we got into the Ban Tong refugee
camp in northern Thailand, there were about four thousand
refugees. The World Vision and the United Nations built the
school in the refugee camp. There were twelve classes and sixteen teachers, including me. I taught in the school for three
years. There were eight catechists who helped and taught religious classes, and a deacon who led the Sunday liturgy.

About once a month, Father Harry Thiel, an American
priest who grew up in Seattle, came to the refugee camp to
visit the Catholic Christians and say Mass on Sunday. In 1978,

the deacon and all the catechists left the camp, and Father Thiel recruited me to minister full-time to Catholic refugees in the camp. On Sundays I did communion service and taught classes. I married new couples, baptized, and buried the dead. My family spent almost five years in the refugee camp. In my family were twelve people: my mother, my three sisters, my wife, and our six children. My family came to the United States to live in Seattle on April 30, 1980.

After I had lived in Seattle for a while, I saw that my people needed help there too. I called a meeting of families from Laos and the refugee camp and started taking the people to church. We went together every Sunday. In 1985, there were about three hundred Hmong in Seattle. I made a list of the people and took it to Bishop Raymond Hunthausen and said, "Here is the list. I want you to take over." The bishop said, "No. I have no one who can speak your language. You do it. I want you to give up your job and work to help your people. I'll give you the salary you're making at your job."

I had no choice. A month later, I accepted Archbishop Hunthausen's appointment to provide pastoral care to the Lao tribal communities. All of us—the Lao, the Hmong, the Kmhu, and the Lamet—came together as community in one church, the Our Lady of Mount Virgin. Our church is home to many ethnic groups: about 400 of our tribal people, two hundred Chinese, seventy Italians, and sixty Native Americans. I was appointed pastoral coordinator to the Lao tribal community, and in 2003, I was ordained a deacon. My job is to minister to all the various tribes who came from the country of Laos.

Our church is the only center for the Lao people. People don't live together in a village as they did at home. Some drive as far as one hundred miles each Sunday to come to church. My role is to be here with the people. I have to explain the culture, the customs, and the rules of the American church and culture to them because they come from small country towns where there are not many rules. I have to translate the information that comes from the chancery and from other places and get the people to understand the culture we need to follow. I have to fit the language so they can understand the liturgy, the teachings, and the documents. Their needs are often the needs of catechumens because they really don't know much about the church.

I try to help families in need. Most people do not have their own home. Many have two jobs. Because they have no education and cannot read or write, they are poor. Their children do much better because they go to school and learn to read and write. They get an education and jobs.

Every day I am in my office and every day the people come to me for help with church matters, such as baptism, or cultural concerns, such as getting a job or translating a document. They come to me when they move, and I go to their houses and bless them. Often people come to me when they have problems with their parents or spouse or children. Whenever I baptize a couple's first baby, I try to finish the instructions on how to raise children in the Catholic faith. Often the parents need instruction too. Sunday is my busiest day because that is the day most people come to the church, so that is the best day for activities. We have Mass at 9:30 a.m. After Mass, we have meetings or classes, according to the individual language group. We try to conduct these sessions in the people's tribal tongue. We do this for the elders who don't quite understand English. Each group elects a leader who teaches topics like religion, canon law, the Bible, and music. Some groups have lunch together after their meeting. All the groups get together for dinner and socializing and cultural celebrations once a month or so.

The biggest problems have to do with the change in culture. The Lao people have to adapt to a new society. Back home, only the parents can choose whom their child will marry. This custom is slowly disappearing in this country. The parents here don't have the same rights and the children have more freedom. If the parents force them, there is trouble. We can't do what we did in Laos. There are things we don't like in this country, but we have to change if we live here. We have to let the children do what they decide to do. I have found that most of the children are continuing to come to church. If their parents have faith, the children will follow.

Another cultural difference that is hard for us is how people talk. In America, the language is more straightforward. People say what they mean, usually. In Asia, people talk around what they mean. There are definite rules about how you should talk and not talk. When you talk, talk around; never talk straight. You don't want to upset anybody. They will often tell a joke or a story to make people feel more comfortable.

This is a big part of my ministry. I know how to talk to my people, so first I listen to what they have to tell me so I can identify the problem. Then I have to find out where the problem came from and what the situation is. Then I talk to the parents or whomever is involved. Finally, we work on how to find a solution. Elderly people coming from Laos don't understand the language and culture. Some of them return to Laos after a while because they can't adjust to this culture. Most immigrants stay once they know the language and get a job and understand how to adapt to the society. Young people don't want to go back.

I spend a lot of time working with husbands and wives who are having problems, but we never talk about their relationship. I can never talk about sex with the husband and wife, and they can never talk about it with each other. This is not appropriate in Asian culture. They will not go to an American counselor because they say they ask stupid questions and ask too much about sex. This is offensive to Asian couples. I try to get them to talk in front of me or someone else, and not just to each other. They will accept or listen to me sometimes when they will not do that with each other.

I have to form relationships with the people and understand their culture. I can help them with the practical problems of joining the American culture, but I also help them get into the culture and especially help them get into the church culture.

Since there are several Laotian tribal groups in our community, sometimes attitudes from home have followed them to this country. The lowland Laotians put down the mountain people. In Seattle, some lowland people will not associate with the mountain people. But I tell them that we are now a part of a new society; we are all United States citizens and we cannot discriminate. The law here says discrimination is a crime and whether you like it or not, you cannot do it. A few Lao families have left our church because they think they are more important and don't want to mix with those they look down on and consider stupid people.

Working for the church and for people is not easy. The people would prefer a priest, but we don't have one who can speak the Lao languages. They have to come to me because I can speak all their languages and I speak English. They accept me.

My work can be frustrating. For me, if I did not have faith, I wouldn't take this job. It's a twenty-four-hour job because people call me when they have needs. I work with so many different tribes, languages, and cultures, and I need a lot of time to do what the people want. Still, many complain. People in ministry must suffer, for Jesus said whoever follows him has to take up the cross. I have to have a strong faith.

Deacon Joua Pao Yang, of the Hmong tribal people, grew up in the mountains of Laos and was baptized a Catholic when he was five. He was educated in a mission school and went to college, but fled to Thailand in 1975 when the Communists arrived in Laos. He felt the call to serve God when he was in the refugee camp. In 1980, Joua came to Seattle with his wife and small children.

II
COLLABORATIVE

Collaborative leaders empower the gifts of all the baptized while working together toward a shared mission. They bring the fullness of the Catholic tradition to the community: communal, sacramental, pastoral, and prophetic. They respect the Spirit that is present and active in the community and in its members.

Four parishes, five churches, three priests

"Gradually, we realized that we had to create our own model of local church."

Father Daniel Lamothe
St. Bernard's Church
Keene, New Hampshire

Parish Profile: Five churches form a cluster with Clairvaux Center as their base. Clairvaux provides pastoral training for new priests and a location for centralized services and offices for all the parishes.

◇◇◇

Our adventure started in Keene in 2004 when the bishop asked me to administer a small parish in need of a priest. I was already the pastor of a large church, but I said yes, if he would let me do it in an innovative way. Eventually, I became pastor of four parishes, five churches, and two other priests, and we developed a new model for clustering as we created the Clairvaux Center, a place for centralized offices for all the churches and a training ground for newly ordained priests.

The initial challenge was to collaborate and to involve lots of people. I knew that all people are called to ministry by baptism. Now I had to help people make this real in a new context. It's different from the way it used to be. Before we felt we didn't need to involve the people. But I knew we did and I tried to find a way to combine pastoral and parish councils and committees in order to achieve more unity and efficiency.

My clustering assignment was part of a new pastoral model in the Diocese of Manchester. I was one of three priests serving four parishes with five churches. This was part of a reconfiguration process in our diocese looking to a future when there would be fewer priests. There were several options: a merger of parishes, a twinning where one pastor serves one to three parishes, or a multi-parish cluster. I had served as the pastor of large churches and had cut my teeth on adding a smaller parish to administer as my responsibility, but at St. Bernard's I faced a greater challenge. The challenge was to find a way for the people of God to serve the people of God. One of the leaders of one of the parishes insisted that involving the people in reforming the parishes would never work, that it was impossible to achieve. A year or two later, he apologized and told me that it was working well.

At St. Bernard's we worked to transform the parish council into a pastoral council. The difference is seen best in the images of prayer associated with each. The parish council had bookend prayer; that is, a prayer at the beginning and end of every meeting. In the pastoral council, on the other hand, prayer was the basis of every meeting. The parish council focused on the nuts and bolts of planning and managing the day-to-day affairs of the parish. Now, the pastoral council concentrates on the vision and mission of the church, on long-range planning, on the future. We now have members seated through a discernment process rather than election. Everyone comes together, prays together, and each shares what he or she has to offer. A facilitator, not a chairperson, moves the body toward consensus. I saw this as a positive step in the transformation process.

New Hampshire has a strong sense of place. Our parishes lie in the southwestern corner of the state, and we are secure in our long-rooted history and strength. Our nearby 3,165-foot mountain, Mt. Monadnock, is an ever-present symbol of our strength and stability, and of our New England heritage. Our people live and pray in its shadow. The poet Amy Lowell called it "thou pledge of greater majesty unseen." This is the constant backdrop of our ministry, which our mission statement reflects. St. Bernard's is a parish community of more than 1,220 families with a large volunteer base to support the sponsored ministries and to implement the parish mission: "Under the protection of God's love we spread the Good News of Jesus to all in the shadow of Mt. Monadnock through word, worship, parish activities, and outreach. We serve all in collaboration with the interfaith community."

Gradually, we realized that we had to create our own model of church. Central to this was the practical reality that our community of churches did not have the same access to some necessary services and facilities. The Monadnock region is a deanery consisting of eight parishes with four pastors. Some parishes do not have a resident pastor or full-time directors of religious education. Other parish and diocesan programs were not readily available to all parishes. We had to address this problem creatively. Our response was Clairvaux Center, center of light to the parishes. I see the center as a prophetic model for the future church both in programming and in priestly training.

We began by remodeling the large former convent into a modern facility that has become the pastoral center for the community. Currently it houses the Newman Center for students at Keene State College; a faith-formation center that trains catechists and conducts a variety of religious education activities and other formation programs; the youth program for the Greater Keene area; Catholic Charities; counseling services; outreach programs; as well as parish offices and meeting spaces. Because we have combined our resources, we have been able to come up with space to do our work and our ministry. Furthermore, the building pays for itself.

We took our inspiration from the Acts of the Apostles 2:44, when the early Christians served the needs of people by sharing some of their goods in common. Today we call it pooling resources. I see this center as a seedbed for ministry in our parishes and diocese. Some of the smaller parishes, for example, were not able to organize training for their catechists, but now they send them to Clairvaux, where they are trained with a larger group. In keeping with its name, Clairvaux has brought light and newness to the parishes.

One of the unanticipated successes of Clairvaux has been its emergence as a training ground for newly ordained priests. I believe strongly that this model is the wave of the future church. In the days before the Council of Trent, people prepared for ministry simply by working with the parish priest. After Trent, priests attended the seminary for their training and had little practical experience. Now preparation for the priesthood is shifting back to pastoral training in local parishes. There is a new awareness that book knowledge is not enough for the parish priest. In New Hampshire, a priest typically becomes a pastor in about four years, so it is important to begin preparation early. By 2012, we anticipate that the

Manchester Diocese will have seventy-five active priests and 125 parishes. This means that all priests would be pastors, but not everyone would be ready.

Instead of immediately making newly ordained priests pastors, we have developed a program at Clairvaux to train young priests to be pastors. They live at St. Bernard's for four years and work in the field in the five churches I pastor. I serve as pastor, mentor, companion-in-ministry, brother, and friend to the young priests. We live together in the rectory and have moved the parish offices to Clairvaux so that we have a separation between life and work. Noonday prayer is always together, and sometimes evening prayer. Saturday night is guys' night out for dinner and perhaps a movie. It is a time to dress down and relax, and it is forbidden to talk shop.

In pastoral training situations, I mentor them in working with lay people in meetings; sometimes I serve as a kind of referee. I have to help them to listen to people, to work with them, to work out a compromise. As a mentor, I sometimes give them advice such as how to express themselves in a fatherly way in a homily. They also go out to other parishes and assignments. They are mentored by me and other experienced priests; they learn how to work with the parish council and how to collaborate with the people. There is time for work, prayer, and play. The purpose is to give young priests as much room as possible to develop pastorally. I really love the prophetic nature of this program. I feel we have faced a severe challenge within the church and have found a way to respond with grace and integrity. Our priests should be better priests because they will be more equipped to deal with people and the world.

Our diocese is keeping true to what Vatican II called us to do. In planning and developing my own ministry, more and more I see it as centered in the Clairvaux Center and reaching out to all of our parishes. I see it as a ministry to enable the laity in ministry, to train priests for pastoral ministry, and to train all of our people for discipleship.

Father Daniel Lamothe was ordained in 1962 and has served in many pastoral and administrative capacities in the Diocese of Manchester. In 2003, he decided not to retire but instead took on a pastoral role in a parish clustering model.

In Queens, the search is on
for lay leaders

*In a predominantly black, immigrant parish in
New York, the people do it themselves.*

Sister Maryellen Kane, CSJ
Parish Life Coordinator
St. Mary Magdalene Parish
Queens, New York

Parish Profile: St. Mary Magdalene Parish is a small diverse parish in the
Diocese of Brooklyn, New York, the only totally urban and most ethni-
cally diverse diocese in the United States.

◇◇◇

A man named Price asked me the first question at my first
parish council meeting at St. Mary Magdalene on a spring
evening in 2004: "What are you going to do for us?" I could
sense the emotion that prompted the question. Their beloved
pastor of sixteen years had just been made the territorial vicar.
Although he would continue to preside at Sunday liturgy, he
would no longer be present on a daily basis. He also knew
that his remaining time in the parish was limited and that he
would not be replaced. The people were feeling his loss and
were uncertain about the future of their community. They had
never been without a full-time priest-pastor before. They were
gathering to meet me, a woman and a member of a religious
community, who would be their new parish life coordinator.

The parish of St. Mary Magdalene, located in the southern part of Queens, New York City, is small, with approximately four hundred families. Ninety percent of the diverse parishioners are black. The majority is of Caribbean ancestry, while others are African Americans and newly arrived Africans. Fifty-one percent of the parishioners are foreign born. They bring with them all the hope, dreams, and energy of new immigrants as well as the problems. They placed before me one simple question: "What are you going to do for us?"

My immediate response, which I did not articulate that evening, was, "Nothing." This conviction came from years working with several faith-based community organizations, principally East Brooklyn Congregations and South Bronx Churches, both of which are affiliates of the Industrial Areas Foundation. I had learned well the iron rule of organizing: "Never do for anyone what they can do for themselves, never." This iron rule is the flip side of the Golden Rule, which tells us that we must do for others what they cannot do for themselves. I believe that the fundamental principles of community organizing are applicable to parish development.

I did not tell the parish council about the iron rule that night. Instead, I answered with a story from the Hasidic tradition. The Jews of a small town in Russia were eagerly awaiting the arrival of the chief rabbi. Since this was such a rare event, the townsfolk had spent a great deal of time preparing the questions they wanted to ask this holy man.

When the rabbi finally arrived and met with them in the town hall, he could feel the tension in the assembly as they froze to listen to his words. Sensing the situation, the rabbi said nothing at all. He simply gazed into their eyes and began to hum. He started to sing and the people sang along with him. He swayed and danced in solemn, measured steps, and the congregation swayed and danced as well.

Soon they were all involved in the dance, so absorbed in its movements that they were lost to everything else, completely centered on the moment, and at the same time, completely lifted beyond it.

It was nearly an hour before the dance slowed down and came to a halt. Then the rabbi spoke the only words he would say that night: "I trust," he said, "that I have answered all your questions." Then he left the town and he never returned again. But the people had learned from him that there was a great dance in life and that they could dance it themselves.

I firmly believed that all the gifts and talents we needed were present in the community. I saw my role as helping the community to recognize their gifts and to develop leaders. I believe that all real power comes from relationships, and that it is the relationships that we form in our parish community that will enable us to carry out our mission.

I spent my first months in St. Mary Magdalene doing one-on-ones. These were conversations of twenty to thirty minutes whose purpose is to develop a relationship and discover leaders. These conversations are not interviews, but rather the sharing of passions and dreams. I learned much and am still learning much about the people through these conversations.

Conversations with African women made me aware of the difficulty they have in living between two cultures. Their workday, often spent in a professional capacity as a nurse or a teacher, immerses them in the mainstream American culture. When they return home in the evening they are expected to take on the more traditional role that they had in Africa. This often causes tension in the family. One-on-ones also made me keenly aware of the number of hours people spend working in order to support their families. Two working parents with three full-time jobs between them is not uncommon in our community. Nor are single working-parent families. The church was very important to people, but time to get involved in the usual church activities was limited. As one young father told me, "I work days; my wife works nights. We have three children under age seven so when one of us is working, the other is with the children."

A number of people including the pastor had expressed a concern to me about how to keep parents involved in the church once their children had received their first Eucharist. The usual church societies and activities did not seem to work. We had to find a way to enable people to be part of the community that would not become another burden or an addition to a long list of things they needed to do.

In my one-on-ones I usually asked people what the best thing was about St. Mary Magdalene. It soon became clear to me that Sunday morning liturgy was acknowledged as the most important aspect of parish life. One of the gifts that is deeply appreciated and celebrated at St. Mary Magdalene is the gift of African heritage and tradition that is expressed in the varied cultures. This gift of blackness is very evident in the art and environment of our church community. Our sanctuary is dominated by a statue of the risen Christ as a person of color. Our altar clothes, hangings and vestments are made of African and island cloth. Our celebration of the liturgy is also reflective of the culture. Our music and dance ministry are high priorities in the parish, and our budget reflects that. Our choir practices long and hard. We use contemporary gospel music as well as spirituals and anthems. We are accompanied by keyboard (organ, piano, and electronic keyboard) as well as drums and saxophone each Sunday. We have three liturgical dance troops, including younger children, teens, and adults. Our sign of peace is a real greeting and time of hospitality. Visitors are acknowledged and welcomed at each Mass; anniversaries and birthdays are recognized.

Realizing how important the Sunday assembly is to the people and acknowledging the time constraints of the community members, we have made Sunday the center and focus of parish life.

The sacraments of baptism and first Eucharist and the sacrament of the sick are celebrated at the Sunday Mass where the community is present. Using the model of the Rite of Christian Initiation of Adults, we have developed rituals for families who are preparing their children for the sacraments of Eucharist and confirmation. November is the month when we remember our ancestors. The side altar is filled with pictures and memorial cards. During Advent we have a special blessing for all those who were baptized during the past year. We celebrate Black Heritage Sunday and Marriage Sunday as well as Youth Sunday. We share coffee and cake after Mass and other special occasions. On the Sunday closest to July 22, we celebrate the Feast of St. Mary Magdalene with an outdoor Mass and picnic.

Our social justice ministry is called the Last Judgment Ministry. Each month the ministry participants educate the parish on a particular topic and ask for an action as a response. Again, this is done at the Sunday liturgy.

Attempts to offer Bible study and other courses during the week proved unsuccessful. The busy schedules of people did not allow participation; especially missing were young parents. Instead we've begun to develop what we call parish family days. These days, which include a meal, a time of catechesis in different age groupings, activity, ritual, and dessert, are held four times a year. We have found the best time to be Sunday afternoons between 5 p.m. and 8 p.m. Our most recent family day was attended by 177 people.

In a recent one-on-one with a longtime elderly parishioner who has suffered much in her life, I asked her what sustained her in her faith. She replied, "This parish. On Sunday we don't just come to Mass, we have church."

In addition to the development of a relational culture in the parish, I see my principal role as the finding and developing of leaders. Since I am the only full-time minister in the parish, the development and mentoring of lay leaders for ministry is a top priority. The leadership of the parish is not in one person, but in the collective of leaders. Part of my role is to find and develop those leaders and to support the development of the collective leadership. One of the most successful ways to find leaders is through the one-on-one conversations.

I have discovered the hard way that no one volunteers for anything because of an announcement in the bulletin. Most people will respond to a personal invitation, if you put in the necessary time getting to know them and their gifts and talents.

The Diocese of Brooklyn sponsors an outstanding program for the development of lay ministerial leaders. I have spent a significant amount of time mentoring parish leaders in this program. Our small parish now has eight members who have completed the two-year program. Several of them have gone on to a third-year specialization. All of them have taken on significant ministry in the parish.

Through a one-on-one conversation, I discovered Helen. Helen is a retired Catholic school teacher who has a deep faith as well as a great love for children. I asked Helen, who was a catechist, if she would consider coordinating our children's faith formation program. Helen said she would. Helen then enrolled in the two-year Director of Religious Education Institute in the diocese, and she is now certified. Helen in turn encouraged the certification of all catechists.

Price, the man who wanted to know what I was going to do for the people of the parish, recently completed the two-year program. I saw that Price took his responsibilities as a father very seriously, so I asked him and his wife, Doris, to consider developing a ministry to prepare parents for baptism. They agreed, and the program is now flourishing. I also supervised two women in the parish in the diocesan pastoral formation program. One now serves as the coordinator of the Rite of Christian Initiation of Adults; the other is the adult faith formation coordinator.

A young mother, whom I had asked to take charge of the altar servers, recently asked me, "What is one of the things you like most about this community?" I said, "People are so generous. No one ever says 'no' when I ask them to do something." She responded, "That's because what you ask us to do always makes us better people."

In the process of setting parish goals for the next three to five years, the eight members of our parish planning committee engaged in 127 one-on-one conversations with members of the parish. As a result of these conversations and a parish assembly, four goals were developed. The first of these goals is the development of a men's ministry. The first objective under the goal is to engage in fifty to seventy one-on-ones with men of the parish to hear their vision and dreams for this ministry.

The members of the parish planning committee have come to understand that relationships don't just happen. They have to be developed and supported. The development of a relational culture with the parish community will only happen if we are willing to put the time and focus necessary to do the groundwork of building relationships one-on-one.

When Price asked me at that first parish council meeting what I was going to do for them, I answered that "I am going to be a leader." Lao Tsu, the founder of Taoism, explains it well:

The good leader the people revere
The bad leader the people despise
The great leader the people say:
"We did it ourselves."

Sister Maryellen Kane, a native New Yorker, joined the Congregation of the Sisters of St. Joseph of Brentwood in 1966. She was an organizer for the United Farm Workers of America and a community organizer with the Industrial Areas Foundation in East Brooklyn and South Brooklyn. She holds a master's degree in pastoral ministry from Boston College. She has been parish life coordinator at St. Mary Magdalene parish since 2004.

The astonishing diversity of Orlando

*"The biggest challenge is to get people to
understand one another, to respect one another's
culture, and to celebrate differences."*

Martha Gravois
Director of Lay Ministry
Diocese of Orlando
Orlando, Florida

Diocesan Profile: The Catholic population is growing rapidly. Churches are large. The Diocese of Orlando cannot build new churches fast enough. In a typical parish, "There are people from Michigan, Ohio, New York, and people from Puerto Rico, Cuba, and Mexico, and many other countries."

◇◇◇

My husband was a career military man, and I learned about religious education and pastoral ministry in the various military bases where our family lived. The military was like the canary in the coal mines: as the number of priests declined in the states, the shortage of priests in the military became acute. Laypeople began to form faith communities. Many Catholics were reticent because they were always waiting for Father to come. The Protestants, on the other hand, went ahead with building their church communities. We were among the first to train Catholics to be responsible for forming faith communities. As president of the Military Council for Catholic

Women, I also did leadership training for Catholic women at several European bases.

The church also had some adjusting to do. Initially, I don't think it occurred to anyone that laypeople should actually be paid for their work! At first I worked out of my home, with cardboard file boxes. At Ramstein Air Base in Germany, I ran a religious education program with four hundred students, and the authorities finally realized that I needed to be paid at least a stipend. I was also living far off base, so far that all my phone calls to the base were long distance. So I asked for office space, which again, no one had ever considered. They got me a beat-up old metal desk and set me up in the chapel annex. It had no phone connection, so I still had to go to the main building to call people. That was 1976.

At my first civilian stateside parish, I was hired with the qualifier that if they found a religious sister for the job, I would have to step down. Since sisters were leaving the convent in droves, I wasn't too worried, but the insult still was painful. My office there *was* in the main building, so I was making progress, but not much. It was behind the kitchen in the room that had previously been used to scrub and hose down the garbage cans. The floor sloped down to a drainage hole in the middle! Those memories, humorous as they now seem, help me realize how far we've come!

The military experience taught me about being in the world—the pluralism, multiculturalism, diversity, and polyglot, eclectic experience of church were tremendous blessings.

After twenty-some years in the military, my husband retired. Our last post was in Florida, a groundbreaking experience, and we decided to retire there. Our previous experience in a civilian parish had been in northern Virginia, where we were not welcomed. I came there with years of lay ministry experience from the military bases and a master's degree in history but was told I had to be a member of the parish for three years before I could be a eucharistic minister. This experience was very difficult for us because of the military model we were used to. Military parishes are small and used to change. In the military, everybody moves every three years. In any given year, one-third of the parish is staying; one-third, moving; and one-third, coming. People are welcomed and their talents used. Hospitality thus becomes very important in military communities. There is the tradition of the Hail and Farewell party because military people always expect people to go and people to replace them. Change is accepted and welcomed.

Hospitality in the military world then becomes a model for the civilian world and a vehicle of evangelization. This is especially important in central Florida, where an estimated 1,100 people relocate every day. Unlike places where churches are closing, Florida always has new people. A typical parish is not made up of local people; rather, there are people from Michigan, Ohio, and New York, for example, and people from Puerto Rico, Cuba, and Mexico, and many other countries. There is a built-in multiculturalism. In the Orlando Diocese alone, the Catholic population is about 350,000. The churches are large; the diocese cannot build the churches fast enough. In the last three years, eight new parishes have been built. The growth of the Catholic population is faster than that of the general population. Parishes are known as funeral or baptism parishes, depending on the age of their congregation. At St. Timothy Parish, for example, there are close to twenty handicapped parking spaces. People live in a huge retirement community nearby and ride their golf carts to church.

I found that I was a good fit for my parish. I had experienced the fluidity of the military life and understood the necessity of stressing hospitality, of looking to see who hadn't been noticed. I had experienced what it's like to be the newcomer, to be the outsider, so I understood how the new people in the church felt. I was used to diversity and multiculturalism and appreciated their value.

Now, as director of the Office of Lay Ministry Development in the Diocese of Orlando, I stress hospitality, inclusion, and cultural sensitivity. Our office provides a three-year intensive formation program for lay ecclesial ministers in the diocese. The ministers are called to their vocation and approved by their pastors. We also train for such specific ministries as visiting the sick and bereavement, and we train parish staff, pastoral councils, and other parish-centered entities.

In all cases, we ask people to look past their differences. In our diocese, we do not have separate Anglo and Hispanic parishes, and in some there is a great deal of resistance toward accepting Hispanics. We deal with this in practical ways: we try to have a Spanish-speaking priest in each parish; we use both languages in the liturgy; all liturgies include elements of other cultures such as music or readings in Spanish, Portuguese, or Vietnamese. The biggest challenge, however, is to get people to understand one another, to respect one another's culture, and to celebrate differences.

Early parishes in the Orlando area were comprised of mostly blue-collar working-class people. As this population aged, and more Hispanic people moved in, the people saw their neighborhoods, shops, and language change. Within the parishes, different expectations of church emerged. One big area of conflict is the financial support of the parish. People from Latin America, the islands, and Mexico were used to state-supported churches. This tradition goes back to the period of Spanish colonization, when the state subsidized the churches. Hispanics have traditionally not had the experience of supporting their churches as the Anglo community has. Another difference lies in the relationship of church and family. Hispanics typically have a deep, lively, family-oriented faith. They see the church as their home; thus, they bring their children to parish council meetings and other places where the Anglos feel children are not appropriate. Hispanic people bring their children to first communion classes but then are surprised when they learn that religious education classes are offered beyond that point.

Cultural differences are deep and can be divisive. Even the above examples are misleading because, just as there are regional differences in our U.S. culture, there are differences among the various Hispanic cultures. Puerto Ricans are different from Cubans who are different from Mexicans, and so on. We have had to learn and teach that Catholicism is not just about English. As someone said to me, "English is not the official language of the Roman Catholic Church." The situations are better now in some communities, but each church has to go through phases of learning. The adjustment is ongoing.

It is clear to me that lay ecclesial ministry is the way of the future. The model is and will be the priest and lay staff directly involved in running the church. For this, we need trained, formed lay ecclesial ministers who can work in collaboration with the clergy. God's people deserve to be well served. The bishops' document *Co-workers in the Vineyard of the Lord* lays this out well. It takes time for people's minds to change. I see the opposition to laypeople crumbling, but we're all part of a bigger picture.

Martha Gravois grew up in New Orleans. She married and lived in Baton Rouge, where she became a Catholic school teacher. When her husband embarked on a military career, she worked in religious education at the various bases to which they were assigned. After a series of military and civilian ministry experiences, Martha became director of lay ministry in the Diocese of Orlando, from which she retired in 2007.

Standing room only in the Oklahoma panhandle

At Good Shepherd, the parish council
takes the lead.

Beth Hathaway
Parish Council President
Good Shepherd Catholic Church
Boise City, Oklahoma

Parish Profile: Good Shepherd is a parish of 120 families in Boise City (population: 1,500) in the Oklahoma panhandle.

◇◇◇

If you were looking for us, you would find us in the very tip of the Oklahoma panhandle, an area once known as No Man's Land. We can visit five states in an afternoon and still be home in time for supper. But we are more than three hundred miles from our archdiocesan offices in Oklahoma City.

If you dropped by for Sunday Mass at Good Shepherd Catholic Church, you would find our church bursting at the seams. We are blessed by nearly twice as many people as the church was built to hold, so we spill into and fill the hall that opens just to the left of the altar. In 1967, when our church was built, it seemed large enough to hold our small parish of about thirty-five families, with seating for seventy people. A few years ago, we remodeled by taking down walls and building a new kitchen, but it was sufficient for only a short time. Today we have 120 families and a new set of plans on the wall. Construction will begin on a new hall and classrooms early in 2007. The dedication is set for the autumn of 2007.

If you were to look closely at us, you would see that the church holds an earthy, rowdy crowd of folks that laugh a little too loudly as we celebrate life together, and we hold one another a little too tightly as we grieve together. Sometimes hands lifted to receive Holy Communion have worked so hard all week they don't come clean, no matter how many times they are washed. You will hear our babies cry from time to time, and we think it is a good sound, a sound of reassurance that there will be a future for our church.

As a visitor, you will be surrounded by friendly faces after Mass, and you will probably be followed to your car and invited to come to breakfast by folks telling you how glad they are that you came. If you should come on a special day like confirmation or first communion, the church will be crowded enough that our shoulders will touch.

Being a member of our parish means living a life that's really shared. Just about everyone has a job. Our very senior members are our best cooks, housekeepers, gardeners, and greeters. They also check on one another every morning to make sure that no one has slipped away in the night. Our men (often with the help of their wives) take great pride in keeping our church's yard and the ten acres surrounding it in perfect manicured condition in the summer months. Our women (often with the help of their husbands) clean, polish, and shine the interior of the church and tend the flowers in the courtyard.

Working so closely together, we get to know a lot about one another's lives. We can understand and feel another's joys and struggles, and others' lives become very important to us. Lasting friendships are made built on trust, and thus commitment to one another.

Our community of faith has been on a long journey. In 1979, our church became a mission. Our numbers had dwindled and we wondered if anyone but God knew we were here. Then, in the early 1980s, a young priest was sent to tend our little ragtag flock of about a dozen people, maybe twenty on a good day. He had to drive sixty miles just to get to us, but he stepped fully and completely into our lives. He let us know that we mattered. Something deep inside him touched something deep inside us.

These simple things made us feel that we mattered, and we became stronger and more empowered to do brave things to improve our parish, to get serious about our religious education program, even to water the lawn and make the church look alive again. Jesus healed others by making them feel that they mattered.

Our young priest was assigned elsewhere after a few years. Since then, our parish council has become the center of all church activities. The president of the parish council is the de facto administrator of the church. Right now, it's just my turn. Problems, concerns, and new ideas pass through this group of elected members and our priest. A recent crisis emerged when we realized that we were $11,000 short on our building fund money. All of us on the parish council were upset and anxious, wondering where and how we could raise this much money. As she began to slowly walk out of the room, Linda, a quiet, tiny eighty-eight-year-old, said that she thought that if eleven people sacrificed and gave $1,000 each, the money could be easily raised. She rather calmly left the room and came back ten minutes later with pledges adding up to $11,000. She was the only one in the parish who could have done this, and so she did. This is the way Good Shepherd Church works.

Our parish council is the conduit to the priest, who must divide his time among four parishes. He knows everything that is going on, is a part of all decisions, and is available when necessary. This is a critical part of making things work. We have to know a priest is there when we need him.

When we learned that we could stand alone, we began to take steps beyond our church and began to see and respond to other needs within the community. We now have a hospital ministry team and an ecumenical grief-support group. We maintain a food-sack program for hungry travelers, and we have an annual car show that generates funds to buy a coat for every needy child in the county.

Our church is as strong and as present as its members are willing to be strong and present. The church is as compassionate as we are willing to be compassionate. No programs or study groups, no matter how good they are, can ever make us be more than we are first willing to be ourselves.

We now know that our flock at the Good Shepherd Church in the remote panhandle of Oklahoma will continue to grow and thrive and flourish as long as we are reassured from time to time that we matter. We need to know that we matter enough to be looked for when we are lost, comforted when we are sick and dying, and celebrated when we are born. It is so simple one could have missed it.

Beth Hathaway, a Colorado native, has lived in rural Boise City, Oklahoma, since 1966. A longtime religious education teacher, she was deeply influenced by the Cursillo movement. She is president of the parish council at Good Shepherd, the main leadership position in the parish, which does not have a resident pastor or staff.

In New Jersey, a suburban mega-parish finds its mission

"We are moving the parish from a series of organizations to an integrated, collaborative group of ministries with the clergy and laity working together."

Tim McGough
Pastoral Council
St. Gregory the Great Parish
Hamilton Square, New Jersey

Parish Profile: St. Gregory the Great parish is huge: 5,500 families and 16,000 parish members in the Trenton Diocese in central New Jersey. It has a 500-student K–8 school, a preschool, a religious education program with 1,600 students, and sixty parish ministries.

◇◇◇

In June 1995, Father Rich LaVerghetta arrived to pastor a very active, vibrant parish community with many ministries and activities. It was a great parish to be a part of. However, we were not focused on a mission, we were not driven by a vision, and there was little in the way of cross-communication in the ministries. The parish council was task oriented and concentrated on facilities and finance.

Father Rich was a visionary person who created conditions at St. Gregory to allow for a true environment of collaboration to exist between the clergy and laity of the parish. He had help; we have eight deacons in the parish, a religious pastoral associate, and a pastoral council focused on spirituality, not parking lots and bank accounts, and who has keys to the church. The pastoral council provides leadership and guidance to the parish community in realizing the mission and vision of the parish.

Father Rich slowly led a transformation. In 1999, as we celebrated our fiftieth anniversary and began a fund-raising program for our new church, he saw an opportunity to ask the parish community, "Who are we and what is our mission as a parish community, as a church?"

A greater emphasis on evangelization emerged, and the parish council began to evolve into a pastoral council. A collaborative effort was begun in 1999, and through a process of meetings, brainstorming, and reflection that spanned a couple of years, a simple, but effective mission statement emerged:

Our Mission

We, the Church of St. Gregory the Great, live as a community of faith called by God and empowered by the Holy Spirit to form disciples of Jesus Christ.

Once the parish mission became clear, to form disciples of Christ, the pastoral council was prepared to take on a new role of being a visionary body that provided spiritual leadership and guidance to the members of the parish through the sixty ministries. The pastoral council became more and more a faith-sharing community that prayed together, shared faith at the meetings, and reflected on its role in the parish. During the transformation there were those who had been around a long time wondering what happened to the task-oriented agendas of the past, and what all this spiritual stuff had to do with a parish council. There were conflicts for sure, but Father Rich and a growing number of new pastoral council members forged ahead.

With an eye toward expanding the mission statement into a series of vision statements, the pastoral council hosted a brainstorming session with representatives of all the ministries. Hundreds of Post-it Notes were placed on a wall with every idea that came to anyone's mind. As we grouped the Post-it Notes, five themes emerged. From 2002 through 2004, we created five vision statements:

Our Vision

The Church of St. Gregory the Great . . .

Is a vibrant Eucharistic community that provides total spiritual, emotional, relational and educational development from the very beginning and throughout one's faith journey in a healthy and beautiful atmosphere. We worship, learn, pray and work together as we become disciples of Jesus Christ.

Is a home where parishioners, empowered by the Holy Spirit, generously give of their time, talents and treasure through regular participation in all aspects of parish life. Their special talents, creativity and treasure make this parish a special place of continuous growth and spiritual renewal.

Is a welcoming parish where everyone cheerfully greets, embraces, knows, and reaches out to one another within and outside our community.

Is an integral part of life in Hamilton Square, Robbinsville and our neighboring communities as well as the Diocese of Trenton. As children of God, we are sensitive to the realities of our world such as hunger, war, homelessness, poverty, joblessness and injustice. We address these issues through prayer, education, and visible actions of justice, peace, mercy and love.

Has energetic, visible, involved and accountable pastoral leadership supported by lay leaders who together constantly strive to meet the spiritual and temporal needs of our parish community.

In 2004, we began to incorporate the mission and vision of the parish into our everyday lives through the pastoral council leadership of the sixty ministries. The model developed to lead these efforts was the circle of ministries.

Twice a year, representatives from each of the sixty ministries gather together. We focus on one of the five vision statements and ask, "How are we in our individual ministries, and in our group, our ministry board, bringing that vision statement to life and applying it to all we do in the parish?"

We made some mistakes implementing this process. At the very first ministry board meeting, we tried to introduce the whole concept. It was a complete failure because we absolutely overwhelmed the crowd. We learned over time. People in the ministries began to see the connection between their work and the mission of the parish. We were very satisfied when we completed the cycle in May 2007. We now have a vision committee in the parish that is developing innovative ideas to bring the mission and vision to all parishioners, and in particular to those who may be on the fringe of wanting to be active disciples of Christ.

A challenge we have faced is ownership of the ministries. Many of these ministries existed long before the pastoral council came along with this program. Some have a tendency to think that the ministry they lead belongs to them. We are working on creating an understanding that the ministries belong to the church, not to any one person. We are moving the parish from a series of organizations to an integrated, collaborative group of ministries with the clergy and laity working together.

A priest friend from Baltimore once asked me, "What you have sounds great, but what happens when your current pastor leaves?" He caught me a bit off guard, and I replied, "Nothing, we will carry on."

But his question stayed with me. It began to worry me. Would another pastor come in and shut this whole operation down? I had heard of parishes where lay involvement was limited to doing the altar linens. I put this concern on the agenda at the next pastoral council meeting, and we had a spirited discussion. Finally, Father Rich said, "If, when I leave, you do not carry this mission and vision on, then I have failed to do my job. I am not this church, all of you are."

In fact, Father Rich was assigned to another parish. Our new pastor embraces the idea of lay leadership and has been very supportive of continuing our evangelization of the mission and vision.

At St. Gregory's, we have witnessed the results of an environment of collaboration, and I am even more convinced that the future of the Catholic Church lies in a collaboration and mutual respect between the clergy and laity in our parishes.

Tim McGough has been at St. Gregory the Great for eighteen years and recently completed his tour as chair of the pastoral council. He continues to serve on the pastoral council. As his term as chair of the pastoral council was ending, Tim began a new venture and was elected a councilman in his township.

III
ETHICAL

Ethical leaders respect the dignity of the person. They are faithful to the gospel and to the mission and ministry of Jesus. They exhibit appropriate behavior in both the personal and the professional arenas.

In a Kentucky parish, pastoral leaders find common ground

"I went to St. John's with fear and trepidation."

"Before I met Father Philip, I was concerned."

Sister Justina Heneghan, RSM
Pastoral Administrator
St. John the Apostle Church
Brandenburg, Kentucky

Father Philip Erickson
Canonical Minister
St. John the Apostle Church
Brandenburg, Kentucky

Parish Profile: St. John the Apostle Church traces its history to the early nineteenth century. It currently serves about six hundred families in the small city of Brandenburg, located on the Ohio River about fifty miles southwest of Louisville.

◇◇◇

Father Philip: As a recently ordained priest in 1998, I was assigned to spend four months at St. John the Apostle Church, where the pastor had been reassigned and Sister Justina had been appointed pastoral administrator. I was to serve as canonical minister for the summer until I left for canon law studies in Rome. I was not looking forward to this position because I had just come from being an associate under a difficult pastor and I had heard that Sister was close with this pastor. I found out later that this was not true. I went to St. John's with fear and trepidation. As I later described to a friend, my arrival was like a clown car at a circus when the doors opened up.

Sister Justina: Three weeks before clergy assignments, I was working in the Office of Planning in the Archdiocese of Louisville when I learned I was to be assigned as pastoral administrator of St. John the Apostle. The parish was informed of this without preparation and the people were up in arms. St. John's was a parish of 650 families with a small school. The parishioners included families, retired military, and older people living in gated communities. Much of the hostility was directed toward me. The people were angry because they were not getting a pastor and felt they were considered second-class citizens. They said that the former pastor had promised they would get a priest. Some of them told me that if I had said no to the appointment, the bishop would have given them a priest. Some asked me what I was doing there since I was only a woman. Adding to the uncertainty, due to the suddenness of the appointment, a canonical minister had not been assigned. Father Philip Erickson, a young priest, was asked to fill in temporarily.

Father Philip: I had no particular preconceived notions about Sister Justina, but I was skittish about how we would get along. She was a member of the Religious Sisters of Mercy, a community known to be fairly liberal. I had no idea how she would accept a young priest as an associate. In our first conversations, it became clear to me that we came from different ecclesiastical backgrounds.

Sister Justina: When I first met Father Philip, I was taken aback by the fact that he was wearing a cassock. This reminded me of a different era, one that I wanted to forget in many ways, one that had some bad memories of clerics and church. I approached him cautiously, wondering how things would go. I was afraid that we might be moving backward.

Father Philip: I wear my collar all the time. I wear my cassock and alb at appropriate occasions such as weddings and funerals and liturgical celebrations. Some people presume certain positions on my part when they see me in traditional garb, but I see this as part of who I am. I knew and Sister knew that my assignment was short term and that we had to work together. We also knew that the community needed healing. I was committed to doing the best I could do during my time there.

Sister Justina: When we began to talk to each other, we discovered that we were both committed to the good of the people. This conviction became the basis for our relationship. We worked out a model for our joint ministry and literally stood shoulder to shoulder. Father Philip and I worked from a three-pronged pastoral model of presbyterate moderator, sacramental moderator, and pastoral administrator. During that first summer, we had two major crises: teenage deaths and an anencephalic baby. We worked hard to show the families that they would be cared for. Father Philip was always there standing with me. Other pastoral entries opened. On one occasion, a woman was dying and her family, who had not been to church for a while and didn't know that there wasn't a priest, called for a priest. I was able to visit the woman. When she died, the family asked if I could do the funeral. Afterward, the husband came to talk to me as a pastor.

Father Philip: We knew we had different ideas about pastoral care and ecclesiology, but we made a decision early on to stay together. Lots of concerns immediately began to dissipate. We realized that we made decisions differently, but that ultimately we came to the same place. Sister Justina was more practical and experiential, and I was more theoretical. She was very clear that the priestly ministry was mine, and I was equally clear that the administrative ministry was hers. We shared pastoral concerns. For example, in marriage preparation classes, we both met with the couple. I met with them initially to get their story and assist them in filling out the Freedom to Marry forms. Then Sister Justina would work with them through the rest of the process. We divided pastoral moments so that each played to our strengths.

Sister Justina: Our model required a great deal of communication. We met weekly after Mass on Friday to review pastoral care issues. It was helpful for me to talk about the administrative concerns and problems in the parish. We shared stories and helped each other to resolve problems. At first, people would automatically go to the priest for everything, but Father Philip educated them. People would bring him announcements at the last minute, for example, and he would tell them that he would be happy to make the announcement if Sister Justina approves it. Then they would have to come to me. It didn't take long for the message to get across.

Father Philip: It was very helpful for me to learn about parish issues and to work on them with Sister Justina. I learned more about how to be a pastor from her than anything else. She helped me in this, my first assignment, and what I learned there has been helpful now when I am pastor of two churches.

Sister Justina: Fortunately, the parish had some good leaders and we began working together. The deacon asked me what I wanted from him. I answered that I wanted a partnership between his gifts and my gifts. I knew that the most immediate need of the parish was an all-purpose building, which would be a million-dollar project. We identified six men who were the current parish leaders and we held our first meeting. At the first meeting, the men grilled me. At the second meeting, they grilled one another. After the second night, a group formed. I have never seen a group form like that. They became the catalyst for the parish and talked to them as a group. They were open and willing to move, and the parish took off from there. The meetings began in August and the building was completed two years later.

Father Philip: After my canonical studies, I returned to St. John's for four more years. Sister Justina and I continued to develop our ministry model and we continued to work well together. Some people were surprised, considering our differences, to see us together. All of us have assumptions, and I can see how people would think this way, because I too had these questions and assumptions at the beginning.

Sister Justina: During the two years that Father Philip was at school, the sacramental moderator was a well-intentioned priest who did not understand the model and thought he was my boss. On the day of my formal installation as pastoral administrator, it dawned on him that he was not the boss. Accepting and understanding the new model of parish has been difficult not only for the clergy but also for some of the members of the parish. Some parishioners tried through the years to question or complain to the canonical pastor. He was always supportive of me and would back me up when appropriate. Most people, though guarded and questioning in the beginning, grew supportive and in the end appreciative of how well the model worked for them.

I never asked anybody for help that didn't give it. I grew and I felt the parish grew during those years in its sense of church, in an appreciation of differences, and in the reality of community.

Father Philip: When Sister Justina and I left St. John's, we received a letter from a parishioner that was representative of the comments we heard from many others. I feel it gives testimony to the ministry we worked so hard to fulfill:

> *Six years ago when you came, we were in turmoil. Many of us were angry, some hurt, and most of us afraid for the future of our parish. Those of us who had worked to build St. John the Apostle from a mission to a parish with a school felt unprepared to function without a 24/7 parish priest. The old model of the priest as the do-everything person and the fierce pride in our parish, along with the uncertainty of our ability to hand on the faith, left many blaming the two of you for our fears. Those of us who did not focus on you blamed the archbishop. Glory be! With your love, direction, role modeling, and teaching we have come a long way!*

Sister Justina Heneghan entered the Religious Sisters of Mercy after high school and served as a teacher and principal for many years. She then served in various roles in the Archdiocese of Louisville, the longest as director of parish leadership development from 1989 to 1998. In 1998, she became pastoral administrator of St. John the Apostle Church in Brandenburg. She is currently working in the Office of Personnel and Planning.

Father Philip Erickson is a native of Louisville, Kentucky, and was ordained in the Archdiocese of Louisville. After studying canon law in Rome, he became adjutant judicial vicar for the metropolitan tribunal of the archdiocese. Father Philip also serves as the pastor of two parishes, St. Thomas More and Our Lady of Mount Carmel.

Forging a common vision in Detroit

"People did their own thing. Whoever had the biggest key ring had the power. We wanted to change the model."

Faith Offman
Associate Director for Family Ministry
St. Robert Bellarmine Church
Redford, Michigan

Parish Profile: St. Robert Bellarmine Church is a historically Polish parish in Redford, Michigan, in the Archdiocese of Detroit. It has a very active Christian service ministry.

◇◇◇

There was no job description for the role of pastoral associate for Christian service when I took the job in 1986 at St. Robert Bellarmine Parish in Redford, Michigan. It included grief ministry, communion to the homebound, parish nurse, adult education, social teachings, outreach to the poor, funeral luncheons, going beyond parish borders, and everything else. I knew I couldn't do it alone or in isolation. I had to talk to the director of religious education, the principal of the school, and the parish secretary, and anyone else who had a function within the church. The pastor was a wonderful man, but he hated meetings and small talk and engaged in an ongoing battle with the disease of alcoholism. I had to build bridges with them all. I soon learned with the pastor that if I did my homework and requested a specific amount of his time, we could have focused discussions about issues, programs, or ministries and begin to implement things. I also learned that the staff needed to talk, so we began regular meetings without the pastor. We needed to build trust among ourselves. At some point, the pastor realized something and started to join our meetings. We realized that we all had to do this together.

As I became more visible and my role in the parish grew, some people became more resistant. One man said to me, "We love you, you're wonderful, but women don't belong in church." The parish was founded in 1954, and the founding pastor did not embrace the Second Vatican Council or implement many of the changes. The second pastor did quickly implement the liturgical changes in 1978, but when he retired in 2000, some people were heard to say, "Now we'll get our communion rail back." So it wasn't too surprising that they did not understand my position there, that I was suspect. Some called me Father Faith, and, if anything went wrong or there were changes, I was blamed. When bingo began to falter because of lack of volunteers and participants, I became the scapegoat.

Fortunately, the staff supported me. We worked well together when the pastor's alcoholism sidelined him in the years before he retired. While he was in treatment, the staff and I kept the parish going because the associate pastor lived off-site and was there just on weekends for Mass and came otherwise only for funerals. I worked with good people who had good hearts.

I kept going because I knew we had to take the risk. We had to meet and talk. We had to break down barriers. Moreover, we had to talk to one another, know what we were doing, and, most important, plan. We had to figure out how to get the parish involved. We had to be the eyes and ears of the parish.

We worked on changing power alignments. People did their own thing. Gossip was rampant. Whoever had the biggest key ring had the power. We wanted to change the model so that the best keys were the keys to the gospel. Power began to flow from people and relationships. Our parish council meetings began to include study and discussion. We tried to learn to see things beyond our own turf and to see how activities met family needs and schedules. This was painful at first but helpful. As staff, we worked on a common vision for ourselves and then tried to figure out how to do that as a parish.

We did it with town hall meetings. We had speakers, questions, and discussion focused around the fourfold mission of the church. Parish leadership and staff began to read together the study editions of Vatican II documents. Our focus began to slowly shift from *me* to *we*.

Our most effective exercise was one about leadership. We asked the question: If we could have the best parish in the diocese in five years, what would it look like? Each small group constructed lists that were eventually reduced to one list of twelve items. We then took twelve pieces of foam representing each of the twelve items and asked each group to build a church. Each group's church was different, yet all were built from the same foam blocks. The exercise was visual, non-threatening, and very effective.

The parish eventually composed a vision and mission statement. We worked from a positive premise, changing a community often more comfortable with the negative. We challenged people to solve problems.

We tried to empower people to stop gossip. I remember the first meeting with the newly formed stewardship committee. As we talked about time, talent, and treasure, it became obvious that everyone wanted to point fingers at who or what was doing something wrong: "Well, I heard that he . . ." I suggested that we not focus on what was wrong but rather on what was right, where we were succeeding, and that we challenge the negativity and hold the speaker accountable. I said we should be willing to ask, "Were you there, or is this hearsay? Have you talked to the person or are you spreading rumors?" I also commented that if a person has an issue with another, the individual should go directly to the person rather than to the parking lot, that one should walk away when he or she hears gossip and tell the bearer of the news, "I'll talk to you when you have the facts, but I'm not getting involved otherwise." I then refocused on the positive and constructive, and the meeting ended up being wonderful, with many participants commenting, "I am beginning to see what you mean."

In 1998, we restructured the parish council and commissions and held a lottery election on Pentecost, one of the first real elections since the council was appointed in 1969.

In 2000, we received a new pastor, a young, energetic people priest. The ground was tilled and ready for him. I was pleased. For the next six years, we worked as collaborative ministers. In 2006, we both left St. Robert Bellarmine, but the new pastor is building on what we started.

The pendulum had turned gradually, but it turned. People began to see what I had been doing. They started to realize that the long, hard road to a common vision was worth it.

They began to appreciate how their model of church and parish had changed. At my going away celebration, I saw gratitude and sorrow and appreciation for my ministry at St. Robert Bellarmine. I continue to worship at St. Robert's and call it home. It is both wonderful and hard; wonderful to be able to just worship and be a member of the congregation and hard sometimes not to be a part of the staff. I have stepped back and I can appreciate what others are doing.

Faith Offman served for twenty years as pastoral associate at St. Robert Bellarmine parish in Redford, Michigan, a suburb just west of Detroit. Her particular ministry was Christian service, which was the equivalent of Catholic Charities in other dioceses. In 2006, she became associate director for family ministry in the Archdiocese of Detroit. In this position, she is working to connect to parishes and their stories and to construct a new paradigm of the meaning of family within the church.

A journey of providence on Chicago's West Side

"I am gathering the lost sheep."

Sister Joseph Ellen Keitzer, SP
Pastoral Associate
St. Angela Parish
Chicago, Illinois

Parish Profile: In the latter half of the twentieth century, St. Angela's Parish on Chicago's West Side gradually changed from a middle-class parish to a church that served the poor. In 2005, St. Angela and nine other parishes were merged into four cluster parishes.

◇◇◇

In 1976, I was assigned by my religious community, the Sisters of Providence, to teach music in St. Angela School. I stayed at St. Angela Church until 2005, when I retired and the parish was merged into a cluster parish. St. Angela had five resident priests when I started working there. By 1994, we had no resident priest, and I gradually assumed more and more pastoral responsibilities. The parish also became predominantly African American over these years. Anticipating these changes, I attended a certification program at the Institute for Black Catholic Studies at Xavier University in New Orleans, and I was certified a pastoral associate in the Archdiocese of Chicago in 1994.

I witnessed the struggles of a community of believers during the eighties and nineties when white flight began. I experienced the racism that exists. As white flight continued, city services diminished. There were problems with housing, real estate agents, banks' redlining, health care, quality of education, jobs. Businesses, grocery stores, factories, and other basic resources moved out of the community. Residents moving into the neighborhood wanted the same quality of life as those moving out. Definitely all wanted a safe place to live.

I became involved in community organizing. I worked with the Northwest Austin Council in their fight against drug houses, housing discrimination, violence, and other peace and justice issues. I went to court with the council to close prostitution and drug houses, joined them on a "smoke out," which is to gather on a corner and cook hot dogs where drug dealers were selling drugs. I organized prayer marches when someone was shot. I found myself getting involved with prison ministry, drug rehab, prevention of substance abuse, domestic violence situations, public aid, advocacy at the Department of Human Services, and many others. Doing the corporal and spiritual works of mercy is where I find myself highly energized. The African American people have a common saying, "Our God makes a way out of no way."

In May 2005, St. Angela was one of the ten African American West Side parishes that were asked to merge into four. The archdiocese had painful decisions to make in the midst of a very difficult situation, but nevertheless the process of parish merger did not go as well as it could have.

We did not have adequate spiritual preparation for the change. The merging parishes did not have a sense of unity before the merger took place. In a community where the leadership of the pastor is crucial, no pastor was in place at the parish where the merger took place. People were asked if they wished to have full-time paid parish staff, but there were no financial resources made available for that. Transportation became a problem. Some affected parishioners had to take two buses to get to church. This was unrealistic and often dangerous on the West Side of Chicago.

St. Angela was more than just a church building in which to worship God. For most parishioners, it was their family, social life, and a place where the blessing of relationships in Christ had been formed. The church was a sign of stability, a beacon of faith and hope in the midst of the struggles of inner-city life. When creating new models of church and pastoral leadership, it is very important to be culturally sensitive to the worship, culture, and lifestyle of the people.

Since the closing of St. Angela two years ago, many of the parishioners have scattered among different churches. Some went to St. Martin de Porres; some are attending other Catholic churches; a few have returned to Baptist churches, which are visible on almost every corner. Some are still looking for another church like St. Angela. Someone in my apartment recently asked me "Why is it necessary to go so far to buy good meat?" With the closing of so many churches, I wonder if the questions now might be "Why is it necessary to go so far to receive the Bread of Life—the Body of Christ?"

Although I am formally retired as pastoral associate at St. Angela, I asked my religious community, the Sisters of Providence, if I could continue to work with former parishioners during this time of transition. There are many spiritual, social, and economic needs. This has been a very painful time for most parishioners. Pastoral ministry sometimes involves a loving relationship and caring providential presence that brings hope and healing. When people ask what I am doing, I usually tell them I am gathering the lost sheep.

Here are a couple of examples of what I do.

One of our parishioners lost her job. She had three children, a broken ankle, pneumonia, and the gas had been turned off in her home. It was winter and they had no heat, hot water, or gas to cook. The pastor agreed to pay the gas company and I took her to the gas company to get service restored. She entered the gas company ahead of me and was refused assistance and treated disrespectfully. When I stepped up and identified myself as a sister from St. Angela, the problems disappeared and the woman had her service restored. It is astounding to me how being white and a sister can create such respect in situations where every person deserves respect regardless of the color of their skin.

Another time I was trying to get a young woman into drug rehab. All the rehab places seemed to be full. Then one night the drug dealer took her and physically abused her. She called me at home early in the morning and was crying. She had escaped from the dealer and I picked her up on a street corner. I took her to Haymarket, a drug-rehab center and, after waiting until they had room, she entered a six-month program. On the way to Haymarket, she showed me where the drug house was located and I had the dealer's phone number from her cell phone. So the next day I went to the police in that district. The woman made it through rehab and is still doing very well.

I am still a certified pastoral associate in the Archdiocese of Chicago. At the present time I am on the Archdiocesan Pastoral Associates Commissioning Board. Having been at St. Angela so long, I am blessed to know and have contacts with many local and archdiocesan resources. I try to stay involved with the pastoral associates and Office of Lay Ecclesial Ministry so they do not lose the inner city on the radar screen.

There's an African American song that goes: "We've come this far by faith, leaning on the Lord; trusting in his holy word." This brings to mind the words of St. Mother Theodore Guerin, founder of the Sisters of Providence, who once said, "If you lean with all your weight upon providence, you will find yourself well supported." I hope and pray that someday we may all be one church with racial equality, that the richness of all cultures will be shared with the entire church, and that the mission of the church will not be lost in financial statistics and numbers to the detriment of the poor and oppressed. I long to see the day when there will be no discrepancy between those who have money and those who are struggling to exist; that we are truly one church in spite of our differences.

My journey in pastoral ministry has been a very transforming and enriching one for me personally. I have had the privilege and opportunity of stepping inside another race, culture, and heart. I am truly blessed. The African American community has enriched my life with their giftedness, spirituality, deep faith, trust, friendship, and love. Together we have had the opportunity to be a sign of God's providence and loving presence to others. Jesus sent his disciples out on a mission.

They went forth in pairs and had the company of one another. They learned to rely on their relationship to him and to their fellow disciples. The church began with these relationships, and in the end, they are all that we are assured will exist in the church in heaven.

Sister Joseph Ellen Keitzer entered the Sisters of Providence of St. Mary of the Woods in Indiana in 1951 and was assigned to St. Angela Parish in 1976. Sister Joseph Ellen served as a teacher, director of religious education, and pastoral associate in St. Angela Parish for nearly thirty years. She remains active with the parishioners of the now-merged St. Angela. She sees the essence of her role to be one of a providential pastoral presence during this time of transition.

IV
PASTORAL

Pastoral leaders are called to be faithful to the mission of the church and to the building of the kingdom. They must be able to care for the overall welfare and needs of the community, while empowering the members of the community to care for one another.

Sunday without a priest in northern Wisconsin

"The big question still remains: will Sunday without a priest eventually lead to a non-sacramental church?"

Sister Virginia Schwartz, OSM
Parish Director
St. Ann Church
Cable, Wisconsin

Parish Profile: St. Ann Church is a small, rural resort parish in Cable, Wisconsin. The population triples on weekends when people come to the area to enjoy fishing, skiing, and hiking.

◇◇◇

SWAP—Sunday without a priest! It happens here in rural Wisconsin on a regular basis as well as in other dioceses. In some cases, dioceses were prepared for the priest shortage, but in most cases, there was talk but not much action. The people in the pews were not really prepared to find themselves without a priest to celebrate the Eucharist.

In 1995, the priest at St. Ann Church in Cable, Wisconsin, retired. The people were given the news that the bishop did not have a priest to replace him. Panic struck. The people wondered why their parish was picked not to have a priest and wondered whether the church would close. They worried about where they would go to church. Most of all, they worried about what would happen to their close-knit Christian community.

I heard about the situation and applied for the position of parish director. I came with good credentials. As a member of the Servants of Mary, I had worked in a variety of ministries. I had worked with the Glenmary Fathers for fifteen years. I had experience in rural areas and wished to continue in that ministry. Fortunately, the pastor in the neighboring town who would serve this church as supervising pastor and sacramental minister was open to hiring me.

St. Ann's is a small, rural, North Woods resort parish with about 115 households. The population triples on weekends in both summer and winter as people come to the area for outdoor activities.

The sacramental minister celebrates the Eucharist every Saturday evening. However, because we are a resort community, we also have another service on Sunday. This is a Sunday Liturgy of the Word and communion service conducted by me or by one of two trained lay leaders.

This presents an interesting dilemma. In a sense the Eucharist is diminished because the sacramental minister is the pastor of another parish and comes in just to say Mass on Saturday. The Eucharist loses some of its impact if it is an isolated event in the life of the parish. In addition, the people tend to come to the communion service on Sunday because they know me. In a big parish, perhaps this wouldn't matter, but in a small parish, personal relationships are very important.

In some dioceses, the bishop will not allow a communion service on a weekend. The issue is complex and questions persist: Are these communion services good or bad? Do they take the place of Mass? Does a communion service fulfill the Sunday obligation? We all know that communion services are not the answer. We all know that the Eucharist is the fullest and highest expression of the church's life and that the church cannot, for the sake of its very health, ignore the needs of the people in the parish that lacks a priest and does not have the Eucharist available to its members.

The church has not educated its people well on the importance of the Eucharist; thus, the people identify with the leader who can speak to them and relate to them. There are very few children in our church, but for the ones that are there, the model of church is a woman leading them in prayer on Sunday. After the service, frequently someone will say, "Nice Mass, Sister." Often, on Sundays, a young woman who has studied theology leads our liturgical reflection. Everyone is called to serve. We have to get people trained to take over certain roles in the church and to assume leadership.

As the parish director, I am the one who calls the community together to worship, who tries to provide a positive experience for the local faith community. I use every measure possible to give the local community the sense that they are part of a larger church. I use the liturgical readings and prayers, for example. In our diocese, a lay presider is not to preach, but the supervising pastor or the sacramental minister with the permission of the bishop may grant the lay leader permission to give a short reflection, or the lay leader may read the homily of the sacramental minister or the supervising pastor. I always inform the community that the communion service is *not* the Mass, nor does it replace the Mass, but is rather a time when we as local church come together to hear God's word, to pray for one another and the needs of the larger community, and to receive the Lord Jesus in Holy Communion from the reserved species. These celebrations should not have the feel of Mass, and I encourage people to make effort to travel to where Eucharist is celebrated.

The Sunday communion services do provide the local community with the means of preserving in a concrete manner its cohesion and unity as a local church in a local community. In many ways, it also strengthens the peoples' desire for the eucharistic celebration that they are denied because of the shortage of priests.

When I attended the Midwest Pastoral Administrators Conference, I was struck by the fact that most of us were experiencing church with a sense of excitement and enthusiasm. In all cases of the parishes represented, attendance had not gone down and the collections in many cases had gone up. Of course, there were still concerns about money, because without the necessary money, there is no church, and there were also concerns about working relationships between priests and pastoral personnel.

Despite all the positive aspects of a Sunday communion service led by a parish director (or whatever title is used in a particular diocese), the big problem remains. Will giving communion from the reserved species reverse the contemporary sacramental perspective that the Eucharist is an event and an action rather than a thing received? Will we lose the consciousness that Eucharist is first of all something we do, not just something we receive?

SWAP—Sunday without a priest. Is it good or bad? I think it is good in the sense that this is the first time that the gifts of some men and women to lead prayer are recognized and welcomed by the community. The big question still remains: Will Sunday without a priest eventually lead to a non-sacramental church? Should we be implementing this new ritual pattern, or should we fast from the reception of communion rather than distribute communion outside of a eucharistic context? Are we, in fact, just holding our finger in the dike to postpone our dealing with the discipline surrounding who may be ordained?

New models constantly keep emerging. I pray that we're open and able to take the risk to keep the church moving.

Sister Virginia Schwartz grew up in Wisconsin, where she entered the Sisters of Mercy and professed her vows in 1949. She worked as a teacher, then as director of religious education for the Diocese of Superior. From 1980 to 1995, Sister Virginia worked with the Glenmary Fathers in West Virginia, then served as president of her community for six years. In 1995, she became parish director at St. Ann Church in Cable, Wisconsin.

In Montana, glimpsing the future of the rural Catholic Church

How will the church continue in the sparsely populated rural west? "A major part of the answer lies in the formation of lay ministers."

Sister Eileen Hurley, SCL
Pastoral Administrator
Diocese of Great Falls–Billings
Great Falls and Billings, Montana

Parish Profile: Sister Eileen served as pastoral administrator for three rural parishes: St. Margaret in Geraldine, St. Anthony in Denton, and St. Wenceslas in Danvers.

◇◇◇

The Diocese of Great Falls–Billings is vast; it covers 94,158 square miles, or two-thirds of Montana. In 2005, there were about sixty thousand Catholics in the diocese in forty-nine parishes, sixty-one missions, ten chapels, and one station. The diocese has forty-four pastors and parochial administrators and three pastoral administrators. The average age of the priests was sixty. Much of the region is poor. Eight of the ten poorest counties in the United States are in Montana. The state is sparsely populated, and the business of farming and ranching is very challenging.

These data seem similar to those of other rural dioceses. We continue to do diocesan pastoral planning, reassessing configurations of clusters or groups of parishes and missions so that healthy sacramental life and pastoral care will continue to exist. Thus, we must work hard at forming our lay ecclesial ministers, for many will be entrusted with special ministry in their faith communities.

In 1990, I was invited to the Diocese of Great Falls–Billings to lead three small, rural faith communities as pastoral administrator. They were St. Margaret in Geraldine, St. Anthony in Denton, and St. Wenceslas in Danvers. The people of each community were faithful, humble folks who were mostly farmers and ranchers. I lived in one community and traveled thirty-five miles and fifty miles one-way to the other two. Open space with farms and ranches dotting the horizon was all that lay between. The Catholics of these three communities always considered themselves part of the larger context of church, both diocesan and universal.

The transition of leadership from priest to non-priest was smooth. It was harvest time when I first arrived, which meant that not many people were available to meet me, so I went to them. I arranged coffee gatherings at people's homes where neighboring women and men could gather for a short time to meet me. This also gave me the chance to find my way around on the dusty roads of the parish. Thus I began to discover the gift of rural living.

These small rural faith communities are true models of small faith-sharing communities that many larger parishes strive toward with RENEW or similar programs. People know one another well and what one another might need. Whether it is a failed crop, help with calving, or ill health, the faith community is quick to respond. Real faith sharing is encountered daily in lived moments of joy, suffering, or crisis.

The center of life in a rural community is the school and the church. Every wedding and funeral, every sports event or school event, brings people together in town. They are the community events!

A few days before Christmas during my first year, one ranching family lost their youngest son and their home in a fire. Volunteer firefighters and neighbors fought the fire. Food and clothing were gathered. Immediately someone had a trailer for the family to live in. An all-night funeral vigil was held in the church and people of all faiths gathered to pray and be with the family. The funeral Mass filled the church and the parish hall, and even spilled outdoors. The dinner afterward, held in the town hall, was packed.

In the early nineties, the parish leaders of central Montana gathered several times to begin to plan for the future. The four priests, who were also the sacramental ministers for my three parishes, myself, a pastoral administrator, and another sister who was the pastoral associate in the largest of the faith communities, envisioned what ministry in the area could look like with the future shortage of priests and the vastness of the miles we served. The plan we developed was adopted by the diocese and is currently the way the area is now ministered to. Two parishes have closed. Three pastors oversee nine faith communities. One is large enough to have a small parish staff; two have part-time parishioners employed to oversee the day-to-day needs of the communities. Other faith communities have individuals who respond as a need arises.

My first year went well, with the assistance of an elderly retired Jesuit priest who served as sacramental minister to the three small communities. Difficulties arose the second year when three priests from three neighboring parishes became sacramental ministers. Each community now had a different priest ministering to it.

My challenge arose when faced with celebrating major feasts, especially the Paschal Triduum. Each priest had his own parishes and missions as well, so he was not available to us. Our people were asked to travel to the mother parish in neighboring towns for these celebrations. Some can do this, but many cannot because of the distance involved and the demands of chores in farming and ranching.

I see our situation here as a microcosm of the larger church. We are experiencing the pressures of two fundamental developmental issues within the church today.

The first issue is the problem of declining numbers of priests and the resulting pressure this puts on the continuation of a sacramental church. What will happen in the future as the number of ordained continues to decline? Will faith communities be able to celebrate the Triduum, or other major feasts? How do we build a future sacramental church when an ordained person is not available?

The second issue is the identity of the parish or faith community. Our priests have always had multiple parishes in our western, rural farming community. But that farming community is getting smaller and the population is diminishing.

How will the local faith communities retain their identity? We don't want to go back to the circuit riders, but we might have to. It would have to be in a different form, because the old image of the circuit rider does not relate well to the contemporary community. The notion of the parish life coordinator is the same; it is not good or bad but different. People must be educated about the changing roles of the priest, the parish life coordinator, and other ministers, and be given time to adjust to new realities of church and to form new notions of parish and faith community.

A major part of the answer, it seems to me, lies in the formation of lay ministers. Our lay ministry formation program is now more than twenty years old. It gives participants a solid foundation in our church and our faith. Other ministry programs have been developed. In 1999, the diocese and the University of Great Falls (a Sisters of Providence–sponsored institution) opened a lay ecclesial ministry certificate program. In 2004, another program began as a follow-up to the basic formation program. And an ecumenical lay ministry program also began in 2004. The purpose of all these efforts is to build the future church with a firm foundation

Lay ministry goes on whether or not there are priests. Laypeople are working effectively in religious education, home or hospital, parish life, and outreach. Happily, in our diocese, most priests are supportive and the formation programs and various ministries are flourishing.

My whole life has been an organic progression toward forming and living a model of ministry necessary and prophetic in the rural church of the twenty-first century. We do see ourselves as the church of the future. I do wonder what the church of eastern Montana will look like in ten years, when we will probably have twenty fewer priests.

Sister Eileen Hurley of the Sisters of Charity of Leavenworth has been a teacher, religious education director, youth minister, liturgy director, pastoral associate, and pastoral administrator/parish life coordinator. Currently, she is the director of the Office of Lay Ministry for the Diocese of Great Falls–Billings.

A parish in the desert that surprised everyone

"A woman in this role is not the expected thing—nor even the desired one. So I realize that the way I handle my ministry, and the way the people perceive me in that role, is very important for the future of the church."

Sister Carole Ruland, MHSH
Pastoral Administrator
Santa Catalina Parish
Tucson, Arizona

Parish Profile: Santa Catalina was a 180-family mission church in 1988. It now has 1,300 families—mostly retirees and many Hispanic families.

◇◇◇

I became the third sister administrator of Santa Catalina parish in Tucson in 1988. At that time, it was a small mission with no resident priest. Nobody expected our little 180-family community to do much growing since it was situated in the far northwest corner of Tucson, which was mostly desert. For me, originally it was just another opportunity to serve God's people. I didn't see myself as doing anything special in terms of a church that was more and more limited by the number of available priests. Now I realize that what I have been doing is offering the church another model through which it can speak to the realities of parish life in the church today.

Although the parishioners had been used to having a woman as the leader of the parish, many believed it was a stopgap measure until such time as a priest became available. A priest-pastor was so much a part of our personal history of parish life, but those expectations seemed to change as the people saw the parish grow and expand its ministries under a new kind of leadership. Acceptance by the people was not a major issue, although some still continue to ask, "When will we will get our own priest?" People have come to accept a sister administrator and like having a woman in charge.

Both of the pastors I have worked under gave me the freedom to develop this community of faith according to what I strongly felt God wanted of God's people. I have always believed that church is built on relationships of people who share their faith with one another, support one another in need, and continue to give of themselves for the sake of all. Those who came before me began this growth, and it has been my joy to be able to continue it at this place. Most of the parishioners are used to the new paradigm; some have even commented that they liked having a woman as head of the parish because they saw a humaneness, a more compassionate, supportive attitude. The underlying issue, however, remains.

As I began my ministry, I did not always know what was happening in the broader church of the diocese. Because I was not a priest, I was not sent the mailings that the diocese sent to pastors. The diocese assumed that the canonical pastor was keeping me informed. Often we functioned as an independent parish, somehow separated from other parishes, not because of desire but because we were not part of the communications system. After many years, Santa Catalina Parish was finally added to the mailing list and this helped to connect the parish to the wider church.

Other challenges began to happen as the community grew into a large one, with two huge retirement communities moving in. Our need for more and more Masses began to make the priest shortage painfully obvious. Retired priests and priests from other parishes took on Masses whenever it fit into their schedules. The priests were good in being available to assist. At times, I even had a priest or two stop in to see me to ask if they could be of any assistance. The people got to know the priests who would come regularly at a particular Mass, and would identify with them as "their priest."

Growth at Santa Catalina has been rapid since 1988. The original small mission has grown to 1,300 families, 80 percent retired people and 10 to 15 percent Hispanic families. Because of this growth, we became a parish in May 2004, and I was installed by the bishop as the pastoral administrator. This was a wonderful recognition of the work that we had been doing to build our church. We had built a new church, renovated our buildings, and established ministries in education, liturgy, music, and care. We were fiscally responsible. It was also a time of realization for many that this was a rather permanent situation for the parish.

We have continued to grow. Our CARE ministry is extensive because of our elderly people in hospitals, nursing homes, home-health situations, and of course, retirement centers. We are financially independent and carry no debt. Our people are extremely generous. We have grown from one Mass per weekend in 1988 to six Masses each weekend, one of which is in Spanish. We also try to honor specific traditions of the

Hispanic people, including *las posadas*, Cinco de Mayo, novena to Our Lady of Guadalupe, and *guadalupanas*. Parishioners work in the various paid ministries, including a director of religious education, a youth minister, a director of Hispanic ministry, a director of liturgy, a bulletin editor, an administrative assistant, a director of CARE ministry, and a maintenance director and two assistants. We see ourselves as the team ministry people for the parish.

Since 2005, each parish in the Diocese of Tucson has become an independently incorporated corporation. As such, each parish is financially independent but still works directly under the diocese, which monitors finances and insurance and still has oversight of the functions of the churches. The legal structure has changed, but it's pretty much business as usual. Because I am not an ordained minister, I cannot sit on the corporation board of the church I head as pastoral administrator. The diocesan rule is that three seats on the board are reserved for clergy and two for laypeople. Two of the clergy seats are ex officio, one for the bishop and one for the vice president or moderator of the curia. The other clergy seat is held by our canonical pastor, who is also the president of the board. I did not want to take one of the lay seats, which are secretary and treasurer positions, because I feel that we must have parishioners on our board. It was determined that I would serve as an adviser to the board.

The current bishop has been supportive of me and my role for as long as he has been here and has tried to make sure that I was included in what the diocese does for the priests, but I continue to sense that he would rather have a priest as the pastor. My role has included all that a pastor would do: oversee maintenance and future building needs, deal with all personnel issues, maintain financial oversight, be responsible to the diocese for all those annual reports due to it.

I do work with a finance council and a pastoral council, and try to make sure that I honor their thoughts and contributions. It is their parish and they need to have a voice. They helped determine what the new church would be through a series of town hall meetings as we reviewed the drawings for the new worship space. We continue to encourage the input of the people at all levels. And one of the gifts of retired people is that they are always willing to share their thoughts.

I really love what I do. It's the best thing that has ever happened to me. I love the people and feel loved by the people. It's a situation that's mutually advantageous for all of us. I have experienced a great joy working with the retired community. Most are professional people who bring wisdom and experience as well as time and energy to the parish. They want to give back some of what they have received. They have taught me and helped me to grow spiritually.

The fact remains, however, that structurally the church is in need of some changes in order to continue to reflect the ministry of Jesus. What began as a stopgap measure has begun to exhibit genuine benefits. Our parish is a happy parish. The needs of our people are being well met. The adults are always ready to take advantage of adult education programs offered at the parish or at our local retreat center. Many new members speak of how open and welcoming the parish is, of how good it feels to be part of such a community. They often bring their family and friends to the church during the week because they enjoy showing off the parish. For many, it is more than the building where people gather on Sunday. It is a place that touches their everyday lives.

As I look back over my years at the parish, I don't see many differences from other parishes in the diocese. And perhaps that is the way it should be. A parish can operate effectively no matter who is pastoring it, depending on the skills of the one who pastors. It doesn't have to be *only* the ordained minister. We just need to be able to find what is best for the ongoing development of church in today's world. And looking at those parishes that have been able to achieve what Jesus has called community to be may be a wonderful beginning for enlivening faith that can affect a world greatly in need of Christian values.

Today, I have become much more aware of the fact that a woman in this role is not the expected thing—nor even the desired one. Therefore, I have come to realize that the way I handle my ministry, and the way the people perceive me in that role, is very important for the future of the church. I see my role as one that can make the church a more alive community of faith because I see women working with people on a different level from that on which men do. Women tend to be more compassionate toward the needs of the members, while men tend to be more matter-of-fact about dealing with members' struggles. We need both in administrative roles in order to have a more rounded approach to the people.

I feel, however, that the church does not accept my role in any permanent way. It seems to me that the church sees it as a temporary fix for a current and temporary lack of priests. I am told that the continuation of my pastoral administrator's role is dependent on when the church leadership feels it has enough priests to take it back. I would like to have my eighteen years of ministry seen as a model for the future. I would like to think that religious, deacons, and laity would be welcomed into the church at this level not because there aren't enough priests, but because we are all called to serve and have much to offer to the future of church.

Sister Carole Ruland grew up in Erie, Pennsylvania, where she attended parochial grade school and public high school. She joined the Mission Helpers of the Sacred Heart of Baltimore, Maryland, and has taught religious education and held various administrative positions in several diocesan offices. In 1988, she moved from Maryland to Tucson, Arizona, to become the administrator of Santa Catalina Parish, a small faith community outside of Tucson.

In rural South Carolina, a stopgap measure that looks permanent

"A priest in every parish is a good model but appears to be no longer a viable one. The new model has to work."

Deacon John Klein
Pastoral Administrator
St. William's Parish; Ward, South Carolina
St. Mary of the Immaculate Conception;
Edgefield, South Carolina

Parish Profile: St. William's and St. Mary of the Immaculate Conception are two parishes in rural South Carolina that share a parish life coordinator.

◇◇◇

Miss Virginia, the oldest member of our parish, was dying, and I took communion to her on Sunday. If you wanted to paint a picture of the Blessed Mother, she would be your model. She had the most serene beautiful face I've ever seen. I told her I would see her again on Thursday. I had to be in Atlanta for the next two days, and while I was there, I got a phone call saying Miss Virginia had died. I was able to see her on Thursday as promised, at her funeral.

This kind of experience validates my ministry. People give me a lot. If they are helping me grow, then it's my duty to help them grow. The people see me as a leader, even though they understand that, as a deacon, I can't say Mass, but I can do baptisms, weddings, and funerals ("hatch, match, and dispatch").

I came to St. William's Parish in 1996 after serving for three years as deacon, director of religious education, and chief financial officer at St. Mary's Church in the city of Aiken, South Carolina. I was happy there, but I longed to do more. I wanted not just to be what I was hired to be but, given my administrative abilities, to help out in running a parish in the absence of a priest.

In 1996, I got my chance. I added to my duties and became pastoral administrator at St. William's in Ward. I basically run the parish. We are in the middle of nowhere, six miles from the nearest store, gas station, or bank. The people there had no priest in residence, only a canonical pastor who came to say Mass on Sunday, and they had no idea what a deacon was or what he did. In spite of that, by and large, they accepted me. There was a man who said, "I'll be damned if a woman is ever going to live in this rectory." Today he and his family are some of our best friends.

At St. William's, I have developed a special rapport with Mexican parishioners. Many have asked me to baptize their children, even though a Spanish-speaking priest was available, because I am with them regularly. Several years ago, the Catholic Extension Society heard about the many baptisms and asked me to stage one so that they could include it as part of a story on Hispanic ministry in the South. I didn't stage one; I had a family ready to go with a baptism. The day of the baptism, the whole church was filled with family and friends.

After the baptism, the whole crowd posed for the cameras at the front door of the church. The picture was on the cover of the magazine's next issue.

The initial challenge at St. William's was that the parish was very tight knit and tended to do everything as a unit. There were about sixty families, all of which (except five) are related. They are the descendants of the original founders of the parish in 1895. Only two families are "damn Yankees." We have tried to put a little more life in the parish by having more activities and more participation by more people. We have improved the physical plant by adding a handicapped ramp, a fenced-in playground, new lighting, and so on. We also have about seventy-five Mexican families and would have more if the church had more than eighty-five seats. Since January 2007, we have not had a Spanish-speaking priest, so I have been conducting Sunday celebrations in the absence of the priest. Although these services are welcomed and well attended, we are looking for a priest. The people want a priest back.

Then, in 2004, I was assigned a small parish of sixty families in Edgefield to serve as their pastoral administrator. When I got there and called a parish meeting, they looked at me with blank stares, not knowing what I meant. They had not had a parish council for ten years. So the first thing I did was to hold elections for the parish council.

In 2006, we celebrated the church's 150th anniversary. We are still in the little stone church where nothing happened, but now the stones are moving. We have gone from 50 to 150 people at Mass, and we have begun to build community. To build it back up, we needed to put more spiritual ideas in their lives. We worked on doing things for one another and for the community. The Episcopalians, the Methodists, and our church together held a steak supper for Katrina. We hosted the supper, and the others decided to give us the money for Catholic Charities to distribute. Community relationships are very important in our small towns. We have good rapport with the Episcopal priest in Edgefield and have gotten to know their clergy and people through joint funerals and weddings. The challenge was to put a little life back in the church. We have tried as well to get family members back in the church; this has been increasingly successful.

I have found that the fact that I am a married man with a family is an advantage in pastoral work. Recently, I visited my old parish in Aiken, and a man came up to me and introduced himself. He told me that a number of years ago, he was going through a bitter divorce and was in financial distress. He wanted to keep his daughter at St. Mary's School, but he couldn't afford it. At the church, we had a fund to help people with tuition. He told me that after I interviewed him and determined his need, and with the pastor's approval, we gave him the needed assistance. As a deacon with a family, I am able to understand that people do have problems. If I can help with something temporary, then perhaps I can help make a person whole.

I hope and pray that we will have enough priests to serve the people. What I am doing is a stopgap measure, and how long it will last, only God knows. I don't see women and married priests as the answer either. It is difficult for a young person with kids to serve the church. A priest in every parish is a good model but appears to be no longer a viable one. If we don't get more priests, I hope there will be enough people willing to work for the church to help it grow. I do not see a return to the old model, much as we would like it. The new model has to work. People like me who enjoy the work and have the energy to do the work are necessary in the future church. Both the diaconal and lay leadership are definitely needed. I, for one, am willing to do it as long as I'm alive and able.

Deacon John Klein, a native New Yorker, was ordained a permanent deacon in 1986. After raising a family and working as a banker in New York, he and his wife moved to South Carolina in 1993 to pursue full-time ministry. He currently serves as pastoral administrator of two small rural parishes.

V
PROPHETIC

Prophetic leaders move the parish in a direction that is faithful to the gospel and toward mission. They are ecumenical, evangelistic, justice-focused, and mission-directed, providing outreach to the community. They are servant leaders, concerned about being faithful to the ministry of the church while at the same time being about the building up of the kingdom.

Hearing a call in Mississippi

"I suddenly realized that God was calling me,
that I was receiving a real call to this ministry."

Pam Minninger
Pastoral Minister
St. Joseph Catholic Church
Gluckstadt, Mississippi

Parish Profile: A mission church for a century, St. Joseph is the newest and among the fastest-growing parishes in the Diocese of Jackson.

◇◇◇

St. Joseph Catholic Church in Gluckstadt, Mississippi, was founded in 1904 by a group of German farmers, including my husband's grandparents, and was a mission church for 101 years. For the past twenty years, we have had three different sisters working as pastoral associates to help keep the community active and growing. Father Bob Olivier, chaplain at St. Dominic Hospital, has been "priest in charge," celebrating Mass on Sundays and holy days. On the Feast of St. Joseph, March 19, 2006, St. Joseph Catholic Church was made the newest parish in the Diocese of Jackson.

In the spring of 2004, we formed a search committee to find a replacement for our pastoral associate who was leaving. Early in the search process, Father Olivier and our committee chairman approached me to fill this position. For twenty-one years, I had been running an in-home daycare business. I told them in no uncertain terms that I could not take on this position. I was not qualified.

Over the next few months my mind kept coming back to the possibility of assuming this ministry. Each time the thought popped into my head, I immediately dismissed it as impossible. I had been volunteering in all aspects of church life since I was a teenager—but this was different. I had commitments to the families of the children I took care of and, again, I definitely felt unqualified.

But God wouldn't leave me alone. Just after Christmas 2004, the chairman of the search committee called again. He said, "Don't answer me now. Just pray about it for a few days." I said I would, but that I still couldn't do it.

I prayed all that day, and talking with my husband that evening, we began listing pros and cons. There were many reasons falling into the pro category, but then my husband, Kerry, reminded me that he was working the night shift at Nissan and I would be working during the day. That was one insurmountable con. I told God, "If you want this to happen, it's up to you." The next day one of my daycare moms was laid off her job and decided to be a full-time mother. Kerry told me that if I really wanted to take on this ministry at church, now would be the time to consider it. My response was that it wasn't a matter of wanting, but more that God wouldn't seem to leave me alone about it. We decided to open ourselves to God's will and see where it would lead us.

I called the chairman of the committee and told him of our decision and that he should put the idea before the parish to make sure that "one of our own" would be accepted. Two days later my husband's boss called and moved him to the day shift. It was a very visible, very obvious affirmation from God. I have always known that God calls people to the ministry—I just always associated that call with the priesthood or religious life. I suddenly realized that God was calling *me*, that I was receiving a real call to this ministry.

In February 2005, I was installed as pastoral minister by Bishop Joseph Latino. I was given all the responsibilities of the pastor, except those sacramental duties and responsibilities reserved for one validly ordained to the priesthood. A more common title for my role is parish life coordinator. It is described in Canon 517.2:

> If the diocesan bishop should decide that, due to a dearth of priests, a participation in the exercise of the pastoral care of a parish is to be entrusted to a deacon or to some other person who is not a priest . . . , he is to appoint some priest endowed with the powers and faculties of a pastor to supervise the pastoral care.

To implement this canon, the Diocese of Jackson has implemented a tripartite ministry wherein the pastoral minister works together with a sacramental minister and a priest supervisor to facilitate the growth and development of a parish. In our case, Father Bob Olivier has been appointed as sacramental minister and Father Elvin Sunds, the vicar general of our diocese, is our priest supervisor. The priest supervisor is not involved in the daily operation of the parish, but he acts in a support role for the pastoral minister and sacramental minister.

My installation began with the words, "You have been given the following authorization by universal law, special rescript, and the episcopal grant of the Most Reverend Joseph N. Latino, Bishop of Jackson." Hearing those words, my first thought was, "What have I gotten myself into?"

I have had that same thought many times since. Using the words *authorized, empowered,* and *granted,* the bishop charged me with duties and responsibilities in three main areas. The first of these areas is the preaching of the Word, and includes preaching the Word of God at daily communion services and Liturgy of the Word services; at Sunday services when no priest is available; at funeral vigils, wake services, or funeral liturgies outside of Mass; at the Liturgy of the Hours; and at the baptism of a child under the age of seven in accord with liturgical norms.

The next area of responsibility is the sacramental and liturgical ministry. I was authorized to baptize children under the age of seven according to approved rituals, to serve as an extraordinary minister of the Eucharist and viaticum and as a minister of eucharistic exposition and reposition, to administer sacramentals—such as blessed ashes on Ash Wednesday, blessing of throats on the Feast of St. Blaise, and blessing of communicants—and to present to the bishop the names of designated liturgical ministers.

The third area of authorization is that of the administrative ministry. This includes presiding over the parish pastoral and finance councils, maintaining parish sacramental records and issuing sacramental documents, preserving and maintaining parish archives, administering parish property, and carrying out all annual reporting required by the diocese.

Presently at St. Joseph, I have an "angel" who comes in to the office once a week to handle the bookkeeping. Otherwise, I am the only person in the office, and I do everything from taking out the trash to counseling parishioners; from watering the plants to advocating for annulments; from typing the bulletin to visiting our sick, elderly, and shut-ins; from answering the phone to attending deanery meetings. I am also involved in the lay ministry formation program offered by the diocese, working toward my certificate in theological studies.

When we were made a parish, we had 110 registered families and one Sunday Mass. After Easter we added a second Mass and we now have 168 families. That was a forty-five percent increase in parish registration in five months. We are one of the fastest growing parishes in our diocese because of the influx of young professionals and the Nissan plant nearby. I anticipate a need for more staff very soon.

The model of a pastoral minister working together with a sacramental minister in the life of a parish is, in my opinion, one that every diocese should begin to implement. It is the wave of the future. It does have its challenges. There are still some priests who are not open to the idea of sharing pastoral responsibility with a layperson; some of the laity have difficulty accepting a nonordained person in a pastoral position. I have been extremely blessed in that our parishioners have accepted me, a layperson and a parish family member, in this ministry. More and more people are coming to me. There are only a few who question my place in the church, a fact that, in the beginning, troubled me. I have realized, however, that there are always people who question, even questioning our priests and bishops, so I try to take it in stride.

I am also very blessed to be working with a priest who truly appreciates this new model of ministry. Father Olivier is very supportive of me, is very quick to point out to others that I am charged with the pastoral responsibility for our parish. He reminds me that we at St. Joseph are a model of the early church, where, in chapter 6 of Acts of the Apostles, men were called forth from their own communities to assist with pastoral duties in order that the apostles could be free to devote themselves to prayer and to the ministry of the Word. Father and I work very closely together in planning for the future of our parish and for the spiritual growth of our community. He teases that "it takes two people these days to make a pastor," but, in truth, this teamwork is vital to the growth and success of our parish family.

St. Joseph could eventually be the largest parish in our diocese. We have a great head start in dealing with this possibility because we are building a team to carry us forward. With the shortage of priests, the involvement of the layperson in the daily life of the Catholic Church will be crucial.

The need to educate the laity on their baptismal call to ministry, the necessity of their hands-on participation in the Body of Christ, is urgent. Most of our people do not understand their own personal call to ministry—I didn't. Most would never apply the term *minister* to themselves. Two years ago I definitely would not have, but now I feel confident in my role and I am continuing to develop into it. My validation is being with people at really important sacramental times in their lives and at times when they need the church in their lives.

We cannot allow our people to dismiss this essential aspect of their call to discipleship by pleading, as I did, "I'm not qualified." We must remind them, as I am beginning to understand, that God doesn't call the qualified. God qualifies the called.

Pam Minninger was an active volunteer at her parish near Jackson, Mississippi, for many years. She initially resisted the call to become pastoral minister but, with the support of her family, eventually agreed to the task. In 2006, St. Joseph's of Gluckstadt moved from its status as a mission church to that of a parish.

Going out to immigrants in Shelbyville

"The emerging model of church for immigrant Catholics is found in the neighborhoods."

Adam Ruiz
Hispanic Ministry
Annunciation Parish
Shelbyville, Kentucky

Parish Profile: Annunciation Parish is a center for Hispanic ministry for the sixty thousand Latinos in the Diocese of Louisville.

◇◇◇

I was in for a big surprise when I moved to Kentucky. I had assumed that Hispanics would be like me, citizens born in the United States, and that there would be only a few in Shelbyville, Kentucky. I soon realized that, in fact, there were only a handful of U.S. citizens and that the rest were extra-legals or recent immigrants. The majority were unattached men, sixty-five percent of whom were Mexicans, but there were also Cubans, Guatemalans, and others.

When I started to do parish ministry for this population, I realized that I had to do some fund-raising. I set up Central Latino, a separate nonprofit organization, located in the parish but legally independent from it, that serves the needs of people. I started with food and clothing as well as job assistance, but

the program soon expanded. It now includes computer training and other services. Mostly, it is a place for people to gather
and be safe.

When I arrived in Shelbyville, I noticed that there were a
lot of guys hanging out at the bar across the street from the
church. I started to talk to them. Between 2001 and 2005,
I did about two thousand home and neighborhood visits as
part of my ministry. Connecting the real lives of the people
with the ministry of the church was key. I learned firsthand
about underemployment, cultural shock, language barriers,
immigration status, domestic violence, alcoholism, prostitution, parallel society. After so many visits, the people began to
trust me. And only in this relationship of trust did stories get
told and the suffering of the people revealed. This is also where
the pastoral presence of a minister of the church became the
most noticeable and effective.

When I started to do that, the reality of the peoples' lives
became clear to me, and I discovered a central truth of ministry in the street encounters. Gustavo Gutiérrez put it well in
his book *We Drink from Our Own Wells*: our commitment
should be to "pitch camp in the midst of human history and
there give witness to the Father's love." When the people shared
their stories with me, they essentially were inviting me to find a
place alongside them in their journey of faith. I also felt, at the
same time, that I was being invited into a sacred encounter with
the Lord, who, in the words of John Moses, is "simultaneously
present and absent, proximate and remote, visible and invisible,
manifest and hidden" in the lives of his people.

I believe that the greatest of leaders are those who are able and
willing to live in communion with those who are different; to

enter into the history and reality of the "other"; to build bridges, break bread, and break open the Word of God together. The great leader welcomes the invitation to enter into the mystery of communion, knowing the confrontation with the "not me" will necessarily bring him or her into contact with the brokenness and giftedness without and within.

What continues to motivate me is a desire to draw close to the people where they live and therefore experience the real questions and the real meaning of ministry. This is true in both the indigenous gang community and in the immigrant community. My work now is with the immigrant and extralegal community.

The emerging model of church for immigrant Catholics is found in the neighborhoods. We are going to discover not only what is really happening but also the organic leaders—those people whom the community names as leaders even if the official church is not necessarily recognizing or even aware of their presence.

Pastoral presence in these neighborhoods is being made real by some very powerful, humble, and courageous leaders. I am discovering that it is, at times, these unofficial leaders who are uniting and leading the community. They are quiet, powerful men, never recognized by the official church. Through the years, they have taught me how to be present to others, to receive their stories and themselves as people. I soon learned to contact them when I wanted to get something done. These natural, organic leaders might not have been formally a part of the parish life, but they rose up spontaneously to meet the needs of their people in lively, amazing ways without formal training. They were to be our energy. We must do the same;

we must do what Jesus did—we've got to do some walking. We should no longer invite the people into our reality but humbly ask them if we can share in their reality. In these neighborhoods, there is a real corporate identity, a real sense that it is the community as a whole that is journeying together.

Oftentimes it is the community that comes to the aid of a neighbor, it is the community that pools resources together to help a family that has met a tragedy, it is the community that together is asking questions and finding answers to the real questions that it confronts daily. I have been amazed at the number of people who have told me about when they first arrived in Kentucky alone and without money or a place to stay, how often they met someone, even on the street, who invited them to stay with them until they found a job or met some other people with whom to live. The Hispanics here have a saying: "*Ven a mi casa que es tu casa*" ("Come to my house, which is your house as well"), and they mean it, because they have a tremendous sense of both community and hospitality.

Most of the men I talked to went to church in the United States but not at home. The church was the only place they felt at home, where their people and language were, where they were safe within their own community. Lots of other denominations were approaching the Hispanic community and trying to evangelize them. The guys learned to spend time at the center with me because a lot of them needed father energy and I happened to be there. They needed *consejo*, counsel. I could father them well because people fathered me well. The church grounds were for them a sanctuary. There is a huge parallel society out there threatening them.

The church needs a new model to serve immigrant Catholics. We have to go out to the people and keep them connected to the Catholic Church and to their faith and their God. They have grown up in the church and missed the right-brain spirituality of *los santos*, candles, incense, and hymns. We need to identify with their religion, their faith, and their culture. The church has to meet its people where they were. This is especially true for the extra-legals who want to remain hidden.

In working with immigrant Catholics, we must face the issues of systemic evil, institutionalized violence, and structural sin. Our work is prophetic in that we stand in the midst of a people, name the reality there, and point to where the Lord may be leading us. Oftentimes it is our own Christian people who have the most difficult time seeing Christ in the immigrant.

I am one of a very few Hispanic ministers serving the Diocese of Louisville. There are sixty thousand Hispanic people (sixty percent of whom are extra-legal), two Hispanic priests, one Hispanic deacon, and myself.

In the current political and national climate, I think it is better to form relationships with politicians and leaders than to rely on advocates. Because we built a relationship, our senator came to Central Latino to congratulate our community, and after that, criticism died down a lot. I am impatient with advocates. Advocates make a lot of noise, but they don't make a lot of difference. Some of them yell and scream and then leave, and the ones who suffer are the immigrants. Some advocates have been helpful, though. Some businesspeople are in favor of the guest worker program from both a business and a humanitarian point of view; some wealthy people have become advocates for immigrants.

I often speak in churches about ministry to Hispanic peoples. I know that many American people have negative stereotypes about Hispanic people. I make two main points to counter that perception:

1. When you don't know people, it's easy to dehumanize them, but when you know them, they become people. You know Juan or Rosa, not just a Mexican. When you know a person, you go beyond the stereotype.

2. When Jesus was born, Herod wanted to kill him. The angel came to warn Joseph in a dream and the holy family left for Egypt. Could the holy family have been the first illegal immigrants? St. Paul tells us that Jesus was like us in all things. They went to Egypt. Did they have papers? We are all like Jesus. We're all on a journey.

Espanol

Trabajo con los hispanos, ayudándoles con todas sus necesidades de servicios sociales y necesidades espirituales.

Hago este ministerio porque soy parte de la comunidad, porque hacerlo es ser un ser humano, es ser cristiano, porque sé el sufrimiento de los inmigrantes al llegar a un país que no es el suyo, perdidos, sin familia, a una tierra extraña, y me siento conmovido.

Creo que el Señor quiere que les demos la bienvenida y les ofrezcamos todo lo que él nos ha dado. Debemos ser testigos de la luz y de la Buena Nueva del Señor.

Pablo escribió, "Alegrémonos con los que están alegres y lloremos con los que lloran."

Somos una familia, una comunidad cristiana.

Cuando Gabriel García Márquez recibió el Premio Nóbel, dijo, "Frente a la opresión, el saqueo y el abandono, nuestra respuesta es la vida . . . por fin y para siempre, una segunda oportunidad sobre la tierra".

Adam Ruiz was born to a poor, large Mexican family in San Antonio, Texas, in 1962. In his twenties, he successfully battled a brain tumor that left him partially disabled and determined to find his place "in this world of suffering." He holds a master's degree in pastoral ministry. He has worked with gangs in Texas and Michigan, and now works with the Hispanic community in Shelbyville.

After Katrina, a devastated parish finds generous friends

"The enormity of the devastation we have experienced is being matched by the enormity of the care and generosity we have experienced from others."

Father Doug Doussan
St. Gabriel the Archangel Parish
New Orleans, Louisiana

Sister Kathleen Pittman, CSJ
St. Gabriel the Archangel Parish
New Orleans, Louisiana

Parish Profile: A thriving, predominantly African American parish in New Orleans with a strong community outreach is rebuilding after Hurricane Katrina.

◇◇◇

In August 2005, Hurricane Katrina changed St. Gabriel the Archangel Parish forever. It destroyed our community. Our church and neighborhoods were submerged in three to twelve feet of water. Pews were floating around. Everything was ruined. We were overwhelmed, paralyzed.

Before Katrina, St. Gabriel the Archangel Parish was a thriving, predominantly African-American, middle- to low-income parish of approximately 1000 registered families in New Orleans. Approximately 560 to 600 people attended one of the three weekend liturgies every weekend. A strong sense of ownership and loyalty to the faith community was expressed in many ways: a high degree of participation by the parishioners in the celebration of the three liturgies; service as eucharistic ministers, lectors, altar servers, ushers, sometimes liturgical dancers, and three choirs. About half the parishioners were involved in more than forty parish ministries, including liturgical, education ministries, pastoral care, family life, justice, and support ministries. Parishioners were very generous in their stewardship, averaging a weekly collection of more than $10,000.

The parish established a partnership with two centers in developing countries: one in Ciudad Sandino, Nicaragua, and one in Latas, Haiti. The parish also supported an extensive outreach to the local poor. We partnered with a local inner-city parish social services center, supported St. Vincent de Paul projects, and provided rent-free space for a tuition-free Catholic school for elementary school students from low-income families. We undertook various other projects for the poor periodically, in association with other groups. In fact, the weekend that Hurricane Katrina hit, the parish was going to launch its Home Sweet Home project in conjunction with Catholic Charities to furnish a home for a homeless family in New Orleans! To finance these commitments to the poor, the parish tithed seven percent of the weekly income to the poor, which amounted to approximately $35,000 a year.

Katrina destroyed the parish. The parish church and other facilities were under floodwaters for three weeks, as were the homes of the parishioners in the area. Almost everything on ground level was destroyed. Whatever the water didn't destroy, the mold did. We were not allowed back into the city until five weeks after the hurricane. When we did come back, we saw a thick gray film of dried mud covering everything: the grass, cars that were left behind, furniture in homes, the church, and other buildings. We also found complete silence: no children playing; no adults talking; no cars driving through the neighborhood; no birds, squirrels, cats, or dogs. Mud and silence.

It seemed an impossibility to imagine that this community and our parish could ever be brought back to life. Most of the parishioners were scattered all over Louisiana, Texas, Georgia, California, and other places. By a diligent search, we found 350 parish families (about half) spread throughout twenty-two different states. A number of families have made their way back to the New Orleans area, living either in parts of the city that were not ravaged by floodwaters or in one of the suburbs in surrounding civil parishes. We see faith and resiliency in our parishioners; we hope things will continue to get better.

Those in the Baton Rouge area (approximately fifty to sixty families) began to meet every other week at the end of September 2005 at St. John Vianney Parish, where Father Doug Doussan, pastor, was located in the interim. They gathered for Mass and for a brief meeting for sharing, information, and support. Father Doussan and Sister Kathleen, pastoral associate, were in contact through e-mail, cell phone, and landline with more than 350 of the parish families. Those with e-mail received a "hurricane letter" with information and support every week. The letter, as well as the list of parishioners and several other important pieces of information, were also posted on the parish's Web site. Most parishioners who responded to a survey say that they plan to return to New Orleans. However, there are many unanswered questions that will, in the end, determine whether and when their return will be possible.

Throughout the ordeal, however, there were always signs of hope and resurrection for the people of St. Gabriel. The parishioners of St. Jean Vianney Parish showed amazing hospitality, compassion, and generosity in assisting the families of St. Gabriel, not the least of which were four wonderful workdays to clean out the church and other parish buildings. About sixty St. John Vianney parishioners, under the capable leadership of two contractors who were parishioners, along with a number of St. Gabriel parishioners, went to New Orleans on three Saturdays to conduct the cleanup.

This made it possible to have the first post-Katrina Mass in the church on the first Sunday of Advent, November 27, 2005, the beginning of the new liturgical year and a sign of a new beginning for the parish and the city. It was a glorious homecoming, with more than 365 people present even though no one was yet living in the area. The second Mass was on Sunday, January 29, 2006. On February 12, we began having a weekly Sunday Mass in St. Gabriel Church, without electricity. Attendance was initially 150 parishioners but grew steadily to 300 by January 31, 2007. By the beginning of June, we had electric power and air-conditioning. While in early 2007, we had forty or more families living back in their rebuilt homes and others in Federal Emergency Management Agency travel trailers parked on their front lawn, most of our parishioners were driving thirty to forty-five minutes in order to participate in the Sunday Eucharist.

A large number of parishioners have taken the first step of having their houses cleaned out and gutted to be ready for the next step when it becomes possible. Helping Hands, in collaboration with Catholic Charities, has helped a number of families with this process. St. Jean Vianney parishioners in Baton Rouge initiated the Companions on the Journey program to twin groups of their parish families with St. Gabriel families to assist them in any way they can on their journey back home. Other parishes around the country have assisted us either by sending volunteers, youth and adults, to help clean out, gut, and put Sheetrock into the homes of parishioners or by taking up a parish collection or sponsoring fund-raisers to send us financial assistance. More than eight hundred volunteers from thirty parishes or other groups, including many high school and college youth groups, have helped clean out seventy to eighty homes of parishioners. Two other parishes have sent delegations to see firsthand the situation and the needs so that they can plan how they might help St. Gabriel. Other parishes, groups, and individuals from around the country have opened their hearts and hands and wallets to reach out and help St. Gabriel in so many generous and creative ways, from sending homemade Christmas tree ornaments, to having an angel tree to donate different liturgical items, to sending an organ for the church, to sending a check every week!

As a parish, we have made the commitment that we will help every one of our families that wants to return. We will organize volunteer groups to help clean out their homes and use our parish resources and the resources we receive from other parishes to purchase insulation and Sheetrock to assist them in their rebuilding efforts. We have also asked for more skilled volunteers who can install insulation and Sheetrock, do painting, hang doors, lay floors, and do trim. The members of the parish family of St. Gabriel are humbled and deeply grateful for all the wonderful assistance that others are offering us in the rebuilding of our lives and our parish faith community. We believe that the enormity of the devastation we have experienced is being matched by the enormity of the care and generosity we have experienced from others.

The people who have helped us are serving in new ministries. Most of the people who have come to us are white people. They are helping African Americans to rebuild their homes. We have been amazed at their generosity and nonpatronizing attitude and feel blessed that so many have come to help. Before Katrina, our church was very involved in outreach. It's our turn to be humble.

We are all amazed at the huge sacrifice made by volunteers. They take vacation and time off from work to come to New Orleans to help. We are amazed at the expense and effort involved in this. Some have had fund-raisers to cover part or all of their expense; others have used their own money. They are a source of hope and solidarity and a sign of God's providential presence and action.

To our surprise, they have experienced their time here as a ministry to them. They have been touched by the faith and hope of our parishioners in spite of the devastation they have experienced. We have come to realize that having volunteers come to our parish gives us an opportunity to minister to them: by helping them experience the depth of the suffering in New Orleans, by the racial bridging that has gone on, by the bond of friendships that have been formed between them and the parish families they help.

This is a unique experience, especially because of the large number of people involved. Many of these groups and individuals have kept in touch with our families, wanting to know their progress toward returning to their homes. We have the sense that a network has been created that binds together all the groups that have come here and our parish families.

Father Doug Doussan has been pastor at St. Gabriel's for fourteen years and was at St. Joseph the Worker in Marrero, Louisiana, for twenty-three years before that. Trained in organizational development and leadership, he has worked to strengthen his parish and to help parish leaders obtain master's degrees in religious education or pastoral studies.

Sister Kathleen Pittman started her career as a teacher in New Orleans but has spent most of her life in parish ministry. She has worked as pastoral associate at St. Gabriel's and before that at St. Joseph the Worker. Sister Kathleen has extensive experience in group process, organizational skills, and leadership development.

VI
COMMENTARY

A theologian's commentary

Emerging models of pastoral leadership

Zeni Fox, PhD
Seton Hall University

In the twentieth century, several images emerged to describe the church: the mystical Body of Christ, the people of God, a community of disciples. Each of them points toward a living reality, organic and communal. Inherent in these images is an intuition of dynamism, of the potential for change—indeed, of the necessity for change. Just as the human body and all social groups change, so too does, and so must, the church grow, change, adapt. In centuries past, when the changes in the world and its institutions were slow, perhaps barely even recognized in a particular age, images of the church could be more static—a perfect society, the rock of Peter. In the twenty-first century, when the rate of change in every arena of life is breathtakingly fast, the ability of the church to change, even while remaining who she is, is affirmed by the very images we embraced to describe her in recent decades.

In an institution as large and diverse as the Catholic Church, it is not easy to name change as it occurs, to describe what is emerging at any point in time. However, that is what this volume allows us to do, relative to the leadership of our parishes, relative to the profiles of ministry in our church. Reading the stories of the leaders we meet in this volume, we *experience* the dynamic of change that is occurring. Pondering the accounts of these men and women, we see that the church is indeed a living body, a vibrant people, a faithful community; we *glimpse* the movement of the Spirit, ever making all things new.

Noting such change, the theologian asks, How is this change consonant with the tradition of the church? Is this change in continuity with our two-thousand-year history? Does this change represent an adaptation in our age that is responsive to the signs of the times and faithful to who we are? These are the underlying questions that I will explore in this chapter through reflection on various themes evident in the stories of these leaders.

A Diversity of Ministries

One characteristic quickly noted from a simple listing of the persons whose stories are included here is that of diversity. We have stories of men and women; of ordained and lay people, vowed religious and permanent deacons; of those holding advanced degrees and those never having finished grade school; of persons older and younger, and of varying races and ethnicities; of individuals from very large and very small parishes, in urban, suburban, inner-city, and rural communities. Further, they hold diverse roles: pastors, parish council members, pastoral associates, pastoral administrators, active parishioners. Some of these roles are new in the church; some can be traced to our earliest history. Theologically, how do we assess these developments?

A diversity of ministries has been characteristic of our church since the first century. In the pages of Scripture, we meet not only those who are more usually mentioned—apostles, evangelists, teachers, prophets—but also many others who are named as involved in ministerial leadership in the church, such as house church leaders, scribes, and even the untitled "those who are over you." In subsequent ages, new ministries and ministers emerged at various times—monks who created monasteries as stable centers of community life and itinerant friars who brought the gospel to the poor; communities of vowed religious who served varied human needs and created institutions to expand their work; canons, cantors, and archdeacons to enhance the celebration of the liturgy. And in this volume, we read of the work of pastoral associates and pastoral administrators of parishes (sanctioned by Canon 517.2), of new ministries in our day, and of permanent deacons, an ancient order now restored. All add their stories to the history of diverse ministries in the church.

Some of these new ministers articulate their sense of being called to a new role in the church. Pam Minninger said, "I have always known that God calls people to the ministry—I just always associated that call with the priesthood or religious life. I suddenly realized that God was calling *me*, that I was receiving a real call to this ministry." Implicit in her story is the role of her pastor, who invited her into the role, and her bishop, who installed and authorized her for her ministry. Sister Eileen Hurley expresses her sense of call this way: "My whole life has been an organic progression toward forming and living a model of ministry necessary and prophetic in the rural church of the twenty-first century." Certainly, the context of her formation and life has been the larger church of which she is part. Patty Repikoff shared her vision: "I was a pastoral leader shaped not by holy orders but by baptism, and I invited everyone to exercise their baptismal call with me." Her consciousness of call shaped her effort to form what she named as "a confident and adult church," contributing to the growing sense on the part of all the faithful that "we are the church." The bishops of the United States affirmed such calls of laity to ministry in their recent document on lay ecclesial ministry, *Co-workers in the Vineyard of the Lord* (2005).

Pedro Juarez, a permanent deacon, exclaimed, "I feel blessed because the Lord is calling me to serve. The Lord is opening all the closed doors." He was persistent in knocking on the door of the bishop, and then the doors of the people, who gradually came back to church. Deacon Joua Pao Yang ministers to the Hmong community, having answered the invitation of the bishop: "I have no one who can speak your language. You do it. I want you to give up your job and work to help your people." Yang said, "I had no choice." Both stories echo Scripture to us.

Sometimes these new ministers create new structures, such as Central Latino, a "separate nonprofit organization, located in the parish but legally independent from it, that serves the needs of the people." This enterprise arose from the work of Adam Ruiz, a Mexican American who learned of the many human needs of the Hispanic people in the town in which he ministered. His story also helps us to understand the value of someone deeply immersed in the cultural reality of the local setting and to see how his ability to offer *consejo* (counsel) to the young men of the community flows from his very identity. The need for ministers from different cultural backgrounds is evident. Other new structures are mentioned, some in the parishes, some beyond, some defined by canon law or the diocese, some particular to a parish. These include ministry board, archdiocesan pastoral council, pastoral or parish council, board of trustees, circle of ministries. These structures both demonstrate and contribute further to the diversity in ministry today and to the deeper involvement of many laity in the life of the church.

The diversity we encounter can also be assessed in light of cultural developments in the United States. One characteristic of our time is that in every arena of work, greater specialization, greater diversity, is emerging. In medicine, many others complement the work of doctors and nurses, including medical technicians, laboratory workers, and myriad administrators. In our schools, teachers work with specialists such as counselors, social workers, and child psychologists. In our parishes, it is consonant with this contemporary emphasis on specialization that some have particular competence in the realm of education (directors of religious education and Catholic-school principals), some in the needs of youth or the elderly (youth ministers and pastoral associates), and some in pastoral leadership (pastors and pastoral administrators). A second characteristic of our time is the emergence of women in roles of leadership in many institutions and settings. The women whose stories we read here hold positions of leadership in ministry that only brief decades ago we would not have dreamed possible.

I was pondering this reality on a recent walk along a seaside cliff, during which I counted seventeen different wildflowers in bloom. And I know that in another month, some of these plants will have faded and new ones will be in bloom. It seems that God loves diversity, that an abundance of forms flourishes not only in nature but also in our church. Why? Perhaps just for the beauty of it all—a sentiment aroused not only in enjoying the flowers but also in reading the accounts of ministry we are pondering.

Full, Conscious, and Active Participation

The *Constitution on the Sacred Liturgy* of the Second Vatican Council described the liturgy as the font and summit of the church's life. It called for the full, conscious, and active participation of all the faithful in the celebration of the liturgy. Such a liturgical celebration arises from the lived life of the community, marking the summit of its life. Such a liturgical celebration also nourishes, like a font, a vibrant community, in which evangelization and care of the least are embodied. The liturgical renewal the church embraced after the council has led to changes not only at Mass on Sunday but also in the life of church communities throughout the week. The stories in this volume are about not only individual leaders but about their vibrant parish communities as well.

Beth Hathaway, a parish leader, described Sunday liturgy in her small, rural parish of 120 families as a truly communal gathering where people "celebrate life together." She also spoke of the service offered within the parish community ("Just about everyone has a job"), and to the larger community ("we began to take steps beyond our church and to see and respond to other needs within the community"). Tim McGough, chair of the St. Gregory the Great Pastoral Council in New Jersey, described the way in which his parish of 5,500 families developed five vision statements to guide the sixty ministries of their faith community. Deacon John Klein, parish administrator, explained, "We are still in the little stone church where nothing happened, but now the stones are moving. We have gone from 50 to 150 people at Mass, and we have begun to build community. To build it back up, we needed to put more spiritual ideas in their lives." Sister Maryellen Kane has a background in community organizing and has a principle, "Never do for anyone what they can do for themselves, never." She continued, " We have made Sunday the center and focus of parish life." Sister Maryellen shared the perspective of an elderly parishioner who explained that in her suffering, her faith has been sustained by "this parish. On Sunday we don't just come to Mass, we have Church." An active social justice ministry is built through the Sunday liturgy.

The story of Father Doug Doussan, Sister Kathleen Pittman, and St. Gabriel the Archangel Parish in New Orleans is especially telling—and poignant. Before Katrina, the parish was known nationally for its development of lay leadership, its vibrant liturgy, and multiple ministries. Its social justice work included partnerships with more than one community in the developing world. The hurricane destroyed the neighborhood and scattered the people throughout many states. However, the parish continued to be a center of ministry, the church was gradually restored, and houses rebuilt, as people from all over the country came to help. Father Doug and Sister Kathleen said: "Before Katrina, our church was very involved in outreach. It's our turn to be humble."

Central to the vision of church proclaimed in the *Constitution* and embodied in these parishes is a dynamic interplay between the building up of the community and the movement outward to proclaim the gospel in word and deed. With very diverse leadership, the picture that emerges is of vibrant faith communities, conscious of their baptismal call, nourished together at the table of the Eucharist, and engaged in evangelization and service of human need in the parish and beyond.

Collaboration in Ministry

Another characteristic noted in the stories is the multiple ways in which people are working together. The principle of collegiality between pope and bishops was taught by Vatican II. Since the council, this idea of collaboration has influenced the church at every level. This perspective has been built into the fabric of the institutional life of the church, since the revised *Code of Canon Law* has placed an emphasis on structures and processes that further collaboration.

At times, the voices in this volume use the language of collaboration; sometimes they emphasize the importance of relationships for effective ministry; at other times they simply embody the principle in the way they work. Collaboration described by these ministers is between pastoral leadership and the people, between ordained leaders and lay leaders, between vowed religious and laity, between the Catholic community and other communities of faith—and even with the secular community. The description of ministry in *Co-workers in the Vineyard of the Lord* roots all ministerial activity in the life of the triune God—the relational life of Father, Son, and Spirit. It further describes all ministry as relational and draws out the implications of this vision by describing the desired relationships between lay ecclesial ministers and the bishops, priests, deacons, and people. The congruence between the emphasis in the contemporary church on relationships in ministry and the stories in this volume is clear.

Father Greg Hartmayer developed a model for collaboration between the people in the pews and parish leadership. "St. Philip Benizi is structured around the pastoral council and its five commissions. . . . Our pastoral council operates from the people's agenda. . . . The people bring to the appropriate commission things they see from the pew and items they perceive as needing action." Faith Offman, in her new role as a pastoral associate, realized that she could not fulfill her responsibilities alone or in isolation and described how she engaged in dialogue with "the director of religious education, the principal of the school, the parish secretary, and anyone else who had a function within the church." She concluded, "I had to build bridges with them all." Sister Justina Heneghan and Father Philip Erickson spoke about their collaboration with each other. They gave an account of the many ways in which they differ—in age, status in the church, ecclesiological ideals—and the fact that each of them was very committed to helping their community. They worked together for a number of years. Looking back on the experience, Father Philip said, "Sister Justina and I continued to develop our ministry model, and we continued to work well together. Some people were surprised, considering our differences, to see us together." Sister Joseph Ellen echoes the vision of the U.S. bishops, saying, that the Church is all about relationships, and although she is now officially retired, she continues to walk with and minister to the people of the parish she once served.

Father Daniel Lamothe, with his parishioners, studied the needs and resources of their region and created their own model of church. He wanted a way for the people of God to serve the people of God. Central to this is a structure, the Clairvaux Center, of which he says, "I see the center as a prophetic model for the future church both in programming and in priestly training." The Clairvaux Center is the result of extensive collaboration, both local and diocesan, and prayer.

Challenges

For the most part, these stories of emerging models of ministry do not name the future challenges inherent in the changes they describe. Certainly, they chronicle the resistance of some, the need for the hard work of carefully assessing situations and seeking creative solutions, the long and patient task of building relationships. But the stories are ones of the successful meeting of such challenges. However, these pastoral leaders name a few themes that suggest work for the larger church.

Some of the challenges have to do with the integration of the new pastoral leaders into the structures of the institutional church. For example, Sister Carole Ruland, a pastoral administrator, spoke of her difficulties of not receiving mailings sent to pastors and of not being on the board of the parish. Patterns of integration of pastoral administrators vary throughout the country, and even within particular dioceses. Adaptation of diocesan policies, and even of canon law, is needed in order to address this challenge.

Sister Virginia Schwartz raised a theological concern about the central ritual of Catholic life, Sunday Eucharist: "The big question still remains: Will Sunday without a priest eventually lead to a nonsacramental church? Should we be implementing this new ritual pattern, or should we fast from the reception of communion rather than distribute communion outside of a eucharistic context?" She raised a second concern as well, asking, "Are we, in fact, just holding our finger in the dike to postpone our dealing with the discipline surrounding who may be ordained?" In each age, the theological questions that theologians and bishops need to engage emerge from the lived life of faithful communities of faith. In our time, the questions raised by Sister Virginia invite, indeed require, reflection, discernment, and pastoral leadership.

Conclusion

The Spirit, ever present in the church, gifts the community of faith with many charismata, including gifts of leadership. The Spirit, breathing freely where the Spirit wills, creates that which is new in every age. Reading the accounts of the leaders and parishes included in this volume, one glimpses the working of the Spirit in our time and rejoices.

Zeni Fox serves as the director of lay ministry and associate professor of pastoral theology at Immaculate Conception Seminary School of Theology at Seton Hall University. She holds a Ph.D. in theology from Fordham University and is experienced in both parish and diocesan work, with more than twenty years of graduate teaching. She has served as adviser to the Bishops' Committee on the Laity and the Subcommittee on Ecclesial Lay Ministry. She is the author of *New Ecclesial Ministry: Lay Professionals Serving the Church*.

A sociologist's commentary

Embodying and passing on the tradition together

Anthony J. Pogorelc, SS, PhD
Catholic University of America

When St. Paul wrote to the Corinthians, he told them that he was passing on to them what he himself had received. From a sociological perspective, we would say that the one who has been socialized by others—incorporated into the formation process that makes him or her a member of the community—becomes an agent of socialization, one who transmits the culture of the community to others.

These stories of pastoral leaders are modern examples of the Pauline experience. They detail for us how that process is enacted today and its vital ingredients. Also, they weave a tapestry that enables us to see the diverse characteristics of those who are called to ministry. Of the pastoral leaders we read about, twelve are female and ten are male. Fifteen are members of the laity; seven of the women are religious sisters. Seven are ordained; of these, four are priests and three are deacons. They span the age cohorts and ethnicities that contribute to the shape and texture of the church in the United States today.

Though there are variations among them, what they share in common is more central. They were formed in the faith through common agencies of socialization. An examination of these agencies has much to teach us about the real essence of the faith the church is called to keep and spread. Such a faith is not simply located in books or ideas that engage the mind alone; rather, it is a dynamic reality mediated by institutions and practices that affect people's entire lives and empower them to become disciples, like the pastoral leaders we read about. Each story communicates how important discipleship is for them and the channels God has used in their formation.

When the late Pope John Paul II wrote about formation for priestly ministry, he organized his thought around four pillars: human, spiritual, intellectual, and pastoral. I believe that these are useful devices for thinking about all ministries in the church. These stories convey the quality of humanity, spirituality, and intellect and the pastoral sense of these ministers as well as how they in their ministries are striving to assist those they minister to in becoming more fully human, sensitive to the presence of God in all of life, formed in the knowledge of the faith and the church, and enabled to serve as ministers. Such mutuality is crucial to the Pauline process of passing on to others what one has received. We now look in more specific detail at these ministers and the agents of socialization that have formed them.

These pastoral ministers have deep roots in Catholicism. The vast majority of them are cradle Catholics. Many of them point to the formative influence their Catholic families have had on them. One layman whose family consists of dedicated laity, a priest, and a bishop sees his current service in the church as standing in the line of his ancestors: "My transition into parish ministry was an honest one, as I feel it's partly in my blood; but as I look back to my relatives, it's easy to see that each generation before me has had to face great challenges in the church of their day."

A laywoman reflected on the pioneer religious spirit passed on by her family, which influenced her entrance into ministry. For some, the extensions of the church through institutions like Catholic school had an important role.

Sensitivity to the importance of family comes through in the way many of them speak about their ministries. Parishes comprising families, in the many forms and sizes they take in our modern world, have an important role in serving families by being a welcoming and supportive place. This is evidenced in the reflections of a laywoman from a rural parish who said: "You will hear our babies cry from time to time, and we think it is a good sound, a sound of reassurance that there will be a future for our church."

A deacon indicated how his own family experience was a resource for his ministry: "As a deacon with a family, I am able to understand that people do have problems." Another deacon reflected on the challenges that his ministry brought into family life: "Sometimes what I do is hard on my family. . . . Sometimes my girls ask, 'Why do you have to be in the church all the time?'" So many of these ministers are immersed in the same challenges parishioners experience as they try to balance multiple commitments. Yet because of this, they can have a sense of solidarity and credibility as they serve others who are trying to do their best as they live multidimensional lives.

These ministers come across as being well developed, both humanly and spiritually; they are strong and mature individuals. This is what enables them to respond to situations and circumstances that they may not have willed or have been able to control. Some stories talk of transitions and the ability to adapt in a creative way. One lay minister, breaking ground in a structure that previously knew no lay ministers, had to muster the courage to ask for an office and a stipend.

We see in these ministers the ability to grow through suffering. One layman shared how his quest to make a difference in this world began with a diagnosis of a brain tumor when he was a teenager. A deacon reflected on how shifting social forces caused suffering for him and his family and redirected his vocation. "When the North Vietnamese completely took over Laos in 1975, I took my family across the Mekong River into Thailand in a small boat when the soldiers who guarded the Mekong's shore went to lunch. When we got into the Ban Tong refugee camp in northern Thailand, there were about four thousand refugees." For another, an act of nature and an ineffective infrastructure smashed a parish and made the need for ministry ever so pressing and difficult: "Katrina changed St. Gabriel the Archangel Parish forever."

The stories also portray people rooted in a sense of vocation that enabled them to dedicate their lives to ministry and to face the challenges and resistance that can accompany it. One laywoman exclaimed, "I suddenly realized that God was calling *me*, that I was receiving a real call to this ministry." That some of the resistance may come out of well-established patterns within the church and society is seen in the incidence of this laywoman who stood up to sexism in her congregation: "One man said to me, 'We love you, you're wonderful, but women don't belong in church.' . . . I kept going because I knew we had to take the risk. We had to meet and talk. We had to break down barriers. Moreover, we had to talk to one another, know what we were doing, and, most important, plan."

A religious sister discussed how structural problems in the church interfered with her full functioning in her ministry: "I did not always know what was happening in the broader church of the diocese. Because I was not a priest, I was not sent the mailings that the diocese sent to pastors. . . . I cannot sit on the corporation board of the church I head as pastoral administrator. . . . I did not want to take one of the lay seats . . . because I feel that we must have parishioners on our board." Another sister talked about the lack of appreciation for lay ministry in some quarters, seeing it as a stopgap measure until the shortage of priests is reversed.

These are ministers who also have the ability to trust providence and the courage to take risks. Even before he was ordained, one deacon remembered how the bishop asked him to change his life to serve the church: "The bishop said, 'No. I have no one who can speak your language. You do it. I want you to give up your job and work to help your people.' . . . I had no choice. A month later, I accepted [the] appointment to provide pastoral care to the Lao tribal communities. All of us . . . came together as community in one church."

Something that came through in these stories was the important role that high-quality pastoral leadership, in particular that of wise and visionary priests, played in the development of the vocations of some of these ministers and in the effectiveness of pastoral institutions. One layman talked about how the gifts of the community and pastor blend together: "The success of our group comes from providing a balance of spiritual, social, and service-oriented activities . . . and from having a pastor . . . who offers our community his complete support." A laywoman in a rural parish reflected on the impact of pastoral warmth and care: "A young priest was sent to tend our little ragtag flock of about a dozen people. . . . He let us know that we mattered." A layman celebrated the vision a priest brought to the community that enabled the development of a collaborative model: "Father Rich was a visionary person who created conditions . . . to allow for a true environment of collaboration to exist between the clergy and laity of the parish."

In these stories, no one sets lay ministry in opposition to priestly ministry. All affirmed that both are essential. At this juncture in the history of the church, it is crucial that laity, clergy, and hierarchy take one another seriously. That means talking with and listening to one another. Competition or mistrust between laity and clergy must not be allowed to fester. St. Paul fought competition in the early Christian communities he served. The vision of priests and laity working together must have dynamism so that it can face the new challenges that will inevitably come in the future. The effects of the priest shortage will demand new and creative manners of collaboration.

These ministers demonstrate that they value and have the ability to collaborate. Collaboration is not only delegation, which can mean that leaders hand on tasks to others. Collaboration means involving others in the entire process of ministry and allowing others to influence oneself and one's vision. Genuine participation means that the vision and mission belong to everyone because they have had input into the process and a role in carrying it out.

One layman described his experience of collaboration in this way: "Our activities . . . are organized and run by volunteers from our young adult community and not by a small group of designated leaders." A priest and a religious sister on a pastoral team said of their situation: "A strong sense of ownership and loyalty to the faith community was expressed in many ways [including] a high degree of participation by the parishioners in the celebration of the three liturgies." A pastor described the model used by his parish: "Our pastoral council operates from the people's agenda. . . .The people bring to the appropriate commission things they see from the pew and items they perceive as needing action." Collaboration requires consistent communication. These ministers have demonstrated their ability to communicate, which means both listening and articulating. As one priest put it: "I started the only way I knew how—by listening and watching."

The qualities these ministers have internalized are embodied in the way they go about ministry. In the spirit of collaboration, they encourage participation in the parish. One laywoman said: "Being a member of our parish means living a life that's really shared. Just about everyone has a job." One priest noted: "The initial challenge was to collaborate and to involve lots of people. I knew that all people are called to ministry by baptism. Now I had to help people make this real in a new context." There is sensitivity to mutuality. As one deacon put it: "People give me a lot. If they are helping me grow, then it's my duty to help them grow." These ministries are striving for empowerment of the people. As a sister commented on her knowledge from community organizing: "Never do for anyone what they can do for themselves, never."

The stories offer examples of how the people are included in the process of formulating the vision and mission. One layman described what was going on in his parish: "With an eye toward expanding the mission statement into a series of vision statements, the pastoral council hosted a brainstorming session with representatives of all the ministries." This sense of vision is oriented toward dynamic action. Effective ministers are able to grasp a vision, formulate it, and translate it into a statement of mission that guides practice. As one pastor said: "We strive to live by our mission statement. . . . In the next three years, we will focus on evangelization and stewardship. We need to redefine and set new goals according to our mission and our developing parish." The leadership exercised by these ministers is done in collaboration with the representatives of the people. As a layman noted: "The pastoral council provides leadership and guidance to the parish community in realizing the mission and vision of the parish."

In the pastoral style of these ministers, there is a profound respect for the person. It begins with how they are able to work together. Two ministers of different generations discussed how they went about seeking common ground: "In our first conversations, it became clear to me that we came from different ecclesiastical backgrounds. . . .When we began to talk to each other, we discovered that we were both committed to the good of the people. This conviction became the basis for our relationship."

This respect is seen in the embrace of the preferential option for the poor. One layman reflected on the situation of immigrants and the importance of the church as a place that shows respect for them: "When you don't know people, it's easy to dehumanize them, but when you know them, they become people. . . . When you know a person, you go beyond the stereotype. . . . The holy family left for Egypt. Could the holy family have been the first illegal immigrants? . . . We are all like Jesus.

We're all on a journey." They realize that outreach is at the heart of the church's mission. As one sister reflected, "In doing the corporal and spiritual works of mercy is where I find myself highly energized." A laywoman talked about the growth she had seen in her rural parish community: "We began to take steps beyond our church and to see and respond to other needs within the community." They also demonstrate a practical knowledge about how to get things done in an effective manner. One layman observed, "In the current political and national climate, I think it is better to form relationships with politicians and leaders than to rely on advocates. Because we built a relationship, our senator came to . . . congratulate our community."

That these ministers are people of substance is shown in their knowledge of the content of the faith as well as their respect for it. They have a concern about ongoing intellectual formation for themselves and, likewise, that their own work is formative of those they serve. As the mission statement of one church puts it: "We worship, learn, pray and work together as we become disciples of Jesus Christ." A religious sister said, "We must work hard at forming our lay ecclesial ministers, for many will be entrusted with special ministry in their faith communities." A priest was delighted with the kind of continuing formation his parish was able to offer to new priests: "Gradually, we realized that we had to create our own model of church. . . . One of the unanticipated successes . . . has been its emergence as a training ground for newly ordained priests."

These ministers have a deep appreciation for the heart of Catholicism and know what is central; they are rooted in the tradition of proclaiming and listening to the word and celebrating the sacraments. Because of their knowledge of the respect for the tradition of the church they are able to identify and discuss significant problems that exist in the church today. One sister reflected: "In a sense the Eucharist is diminished because the sacramental minister is the pastor of another parish and comes in just to say Mass on Saturday. The Eucharist loses some of its impact if it is an isolated event in the life of the parish. . . . I always inform the community that the communion service is *not* the Mass, nor does it replace the Mass."

Someone once said that if you want to learn about a religion, you can study its texts. But an even better way to learn is to study the people who interact with these texts as their scriptures. Knowing them will give you an insight into what the texts are supposed to do. We have read the stories of persons who have internalized their Catholic faith and are engaged in the ministry of spreading it. These stories tell us how important it is for ministers to be well developed humanly, spiritually, and intellectually so they can create the pastoral structures to effectively pass on the faith as a way of life. Their stories also remind us that ministry is an interdependent reality. Lay men and women, religious, and the ordained are meant to engage in dialogue as they strive to envision and carry out effectively for today the commission given them by Christ.

Anthony J. Pogorelc is a Sulpician priest who has been on the faculty of the Catholic University of America since 2002. He is the director of pastoral formation at the University Seminary, Theological College, where he is also an adviser and spiritual director. He teaches in the department of sociology and is a fellow at the Life Cycle Institute. He received an M.Div. from St. Michael's College of the Toronto School of Theology and an M.S. and Ph.D. in sociology of religion from Purdue University.

A psychologist's commentary

Reflections from a psychological perspective

Donna Markham OP, PhD

The case studies on emerging models of pastoral leadership represent a sign of hope for the future of the church in the United States. Examining the cases from my perspective as a psychologist who has been engaged in organizational transformation efforts for most of my years as a clinician and as a woman religious in various positions of leadership, I would like to offer some reflections that may serve to reinforce what I see as transformative leadership behaviors in the pastoral setting. I will also draw attention to some potential pitfalls that could serve to derail the movement toward increased lay involvement in the life of the church.

Transformative Leadership Behaviors

All communities, whether they are small groups or large organizations, respond to the health or to the pathology of their leaders. That is, when those in leadership are secure, intellectually capable, nondefensive, and capable of strong collaborative relationships, group members instinctively respond in a positive manner. The organizational mission and vision take root as significant community bonds are established. Contrarily, when those in leadership are self-focused, doubtful of their ability to accomplish the task at hand, devaluing of others whom they perceive to be a threat, and unable or unwilling to communicate, group members respond with anger, withdrawal, and various forms of passive-aggressive behavior. Ultimately, if the members of the group are able, they typically sever their ties with the organization and move toward more rewarding involvement in some other group.

Contemporary insights from many spheres of academic thought underscore the importance of community, connection, and collaboration if we are to survive as a planet. This demands effective and creative leadership. Those who are selected to lead in this fragile time must be capable of establishing the cooperative relationships that seed any community. Parishes and dioceses are no exception when it comes either to organizational functioning or to the need for excellent leadership. As faith communities work toward an ever-deeper immersion in the mission of Jesus in this contemporary era, effective leadership becomes not simply an intermittent wonderful experience but also a true necessity.

Most of the case studies presented indicate the components of such transformative leadership. What is significant at the outset is the struggle that is inevitable as new pastoral models are emerging. The ability to work through these often awkward and conflicted beginnings depends on the underlying emotional and spiritual health of the parties involved. Some of these struggles include, Whose parish is it? Who has authority to make decisions? and How will conflicts be resolved?

Whose Parish Is It?

Those pastoral settings that seemed most alive and engaged in the mission reflected a strong sense of ownership by the parishioners. Underlying such a sense of ownership is the positive self-image of the pastoral leader, lay or ordained, who is comfortable with delegation and at ease with collaboration. In one vignette, a new pastor found that dozens of parish keys had been given to parishioners in an effort to make it feasible for the people to carry out the various pastoral functions needed in their large parish. Numbers of commissions and a pastoral council set the agenda for the community. It is interesting that this new pastor was clearly comfortable in a model of church where the people took responsibility for their parish and counted upon the pastor for insight, leadership, and encouragement. He knew that the parish was not his but ultimately belonged to the faith community of which he now was a part. His internal sense of security allowed him to function as an effective servant leader, supporting and calling forth parishioners in their competence and goodness in response to the needs of the people and serving them as their pastor. In addition to his secure self-image, this pastor exhibits the ability to form collaborative relationships with his parishioners, whom he obviously trusts and values.

This innate realization of the parishioners' ownership of their parish seems to make it possible for ordained and non-ordained to establish effective models of shared responsibility, although this is often a delicate and daunting undertaking. Beyond the awareness that parish functioning is not totally dependent upon the ordained, the success of pastoral leadership where a non-ordained person is the full-time presence and the priest is sacramental moderator, present on a part-time basis, depends heavily on the secure functioning of both individuals. In one case study, a priest and woman religious with vastly different backgrounds and perspectives on pastoral care were able to transcend their differences because of their deep commitment to the people of the parish. At some level, they both realized that they were there for the sake of the people and that they were there to be of service. Neither was bent on control. Their ability to engage in ongoing dialogue as a means of working through their differences was likely more significant for the life of that faith community than either of them could have imagined. In an age where differences often escalate to silent standoffs or result in the formation of entrenched subgroups and factions, their ability to model collaboration and mutual respect served as a healing witness to a parish that had previously been in turmoil. With their leadership, parish members grew to believe in themselves enough to establish a strong parish community in the absence of a full-time priest.

Who Has Authority to Make Decisions?

When leaders trust that all the gifts needed for the parish reside in the community, they are far more open to engaging in participative decision making, built upon principles of subsidiarity and collaboration. Narcissistic leaders who believe that they—because of their superior abilities—are in sole possession of the right to make decisions cause significant harm and endanger the future mission of the group. Most case studies highlighted the involvement of the parishioners in the pastoral outreach of the parish and made significant reference to the participation of the people in decision-making processes through parish councils and various committees and commissions. Good collaboration between lay ecclesial leaders and the priests or deacons who serve the sacramental life of the parish seemed to make arguments over decision-making invisible.

Those situations, however, in which the lay minister or deacon felt heavily responsible for the parish seemed to give expression to the weight of the leader's role and the underlying hope that one day there would be enough priests to cover the parishes again. As the question, Whose parish is it? remains unaddressed, leaders are likely to feel that decisions, and the implementation of those decisions, are their responsibility. This invariably results in exhaustion and stale functioning. The effective use of power is grounded in good relationships. Pastoral leaders who are not attentive to fostering working alliances with parishioners and encouraging communication among persons of different perspectives and outlooks within the parish will experience the burden of leadership and will ultimately dampen the spirit of the community.

How Will Conflicts Be Resolved?

Transformative leaders know that conflicts will be resolved only with the help of ongoing dialogue. Given increased polarization within a group, communication becomes essential to preserving the unity of the group. The primary goal of any good leader is to preserve the unity of the community.

That happens through a commitment to dialogue. Effective pastoral leaders know that determining what can be done to sustain the relationship with the disagreeing or different "other" is far more important than determining strategies for winning some argument or proving themselves right. The Gospel is filled with accounts of Jesus engaging in dialogue and establishing relationships with characters with whom he likely has serious problems—adulterers, tax collectors, sinners, and nonbelievers. He does not try to convince these people to think and believe what he does. He simply loves them. Love establishes relationship with the different, even faltering, other. Love always outweighs righteousness for him.

The significance of connecting through dialogue has become a field of study for many people concerned about the precarious nature of our world. Perhaps most familiar to many is the work undertaken by the late Cardinal Bernardin as he so desperately longed to help opposing pockets of our church find common ground in the interest of unity. From an entirely different field of study, scientist David Bohm pushes the human community to discover our connections through multifaceted dialogues that illuminate the underlying unity among us. One of the greatest physicists and thinkers of the twentieth century, Bohm wrote in his book *On Dialogue*, "Love will go away if we can't communicate and share meaning. . . . If we can really communicate, then we will have fellowship, participation, friendship and love. . . . Such an energy has been called 'communion.'" While neither Cardinal Bernardin nor David Bohm could have imagined the danger of these times, they each knew at some profound level how essential it is for us to foster community through our conflicts and differences. Love will go away if we can't communicate. Transformative pastoral leaders know this in their bones.

Establishing relationships of mutual respect frees the faith community to manage its differences. It calls for a certain pastoral humility. In listening with openness to the opposing other, these leaders learn how perspectives have been formulated and what experiences lay beneath a given position. Respectful communication strengthens the bonds of community.

These leaders strive to connect people in a positive way, so that parishioners who may have widely differing views about important matters realize that they are all invested in promoting the common goods of life, respect, mercy, and forgiveness. These pastoral leaders call the community of faith to step beyond any determined avoidance of one another.

Moving beyond the separate *I* toward the promise of a connected *we*, the transformative pastoral leader calls the parish to a communion that witnesses to the reign of God. In our accustomed autonomous and often-righteous individualistic life stance, this becomes very challenging. Dialogue describes the kind of conversation that builds a synergistic new and better understanding of an issue, while discussion describes the kind of conversation that only presents and compares current points of view. Dialogue leads to relationship as parties actively listen to understand others' points of view and speak to describe their point of view while working to build a shared understanding (see the Harvard Negotiation Project, Triad Consulting Group, and William Isaacs, *Dialogue and the Art of Thinking Together* [New York: Doubleday, 1999]).

Those case studies that exhibited the most hope for a thriving community of faith included such testimony to collaboration, effective communication, deep respect for the gifts of all, and a desire to extend themselves in service to the needs of people in need. Their leaders possessed a sense of inner security, warmth, creativity, and openness.

A Few Possible Pitfalls and Challenges

The ordination of increasing numbers of men to the diaconate could obviate the emerging role of the laity. More worrisome is the fact that the role of women in the pastoral leadership of the faith community may become seriously compromised as deacons are appointed to replace them. While initially women religious often assumed the role of pastoral leadership in parishes without a full-time priest, it has only more recently become possible for theologically prepared laywomen to assume such positions. For these women to replace women religious seems both faithful to the integrity of religious life and reflective of the role of the laity in emerging service to the church. What is at stake, however, is the demise of the feminine face of leadership within the parochial setting. A credible rationale for the ordination of increasing numbers of deacons needs to be presented, and care must be taken so that these men are prepared to function in a collaborative manner with women—lay and religious.

As more lay women and men become theologically prepared, it is crucial that those who are ordained are prepared spiritually and emotionally to engage in collegial peer relationships with their lay counterparts.

The case studies by and large tell success stories. We know, however, that not all efforts are successful as parishioners and lay ministers struggle to negotiate new responsibilities in the faith community. Sufficient structures must be in place at the diocesan level to assist these nascent efforts to intensify. In addition, training and assistance in conflict management and dialogic interchange needs to be available as an integral part of pastoral leadership formation as it is expressed through ordained leadership and lay leadership. Simply completing a program of studies will not be sufficient to ensure effective transformational leadership in the church today, given the complexities and demands facing us all.

These pages contain enormous hope and incredible opportunity to intensify our church's life in mission in these difficult times. Courageous men and women have presented themselves in gracious and humble service. These leaders live with the deep conviction that, above all else, love must endure and will endure if we continue to communicate.

Donna Markham, OP, PhD, is an Adrian Dominican sister and a licensed clinical psychologist. A clinician, writer, and leader, she has dedicated the majority of her life to fostering the health of the church and to developing strategies for organizational transformation.

The Project: Emerging Models of Pastoral Leadership

Marti R. Jewell
Project Director

From 2003 through 2007, the Emerging Models of Pastoral Leadership Project, a collaborative effort of six national organizations, funded by the Lilly Endowment, conducted national research on the emerging models of parishes and parish leadership. As part of this research, nearly eight hundred priests, deacons, and lay ecclesial ministers, from more than two-thirds of U.S. dioceses, participated in symposia designed to surface current trends and insights into parish leadership. Together, they identified the challenges of parish life today and painted a picture of how to effectively respond to these challenges for the future.

In the process, we met men and women whose stories and experiences touched our hearts. They spoke of ministerial lives of integrity, fidelity, authenticity, and commitment. The stories in this volume are representative of stories we heard from all parts of the country and from every leadership position. In listening to them we began to understand that the future of parish life is alive and well, being shaped and cared for by the pastoral leaders themselves. They provided extensive research data that is available to the public and is currently in the process of being analyzed.

The six partner organizations of the Emerging Models Project include:

- National Association for Lay Ministry
- Conference for Pastoral Planning and Council Development
- National Association of Church Personnel Administrators
- National Association of Diaconate Directors
- National Catholic Young Adult Ministry Association
- National Federation of Priests' Councils

Together, these six ministerial organizations conducted research initiatives in six different areas, including studies of lay ecclesial ministry, Canon 517.2 leadership, multiple-parish pastoring, human resource issues, the next generation of pastoral leaders, and a leadership series that studied best practices for pastoral leaders and parish leadership structures. Information on each of these initiatives is available on the Emerging Models Project Web site, at www.emergingmodels.org.

Pastoral leaders who have participated in these research initiatives have provided significant insight into the emerging leadership of U.S. Catholic parishes. We thank them for their contribution to the Emerging Models Project and for their contribution to shaping the future of parish life.